FROM THE AUTHOR OF **THE TAKEO EFFECT**

2024 PREMIUM FINANCED LIFE INSURANCE

THE KEY TO EFFECTIVE ESTATE TAX PLANNING

DARREN SUGIYAMA

DARREN SUGIYAMA

PREMIUM FINANCED LIFE INSURANCE

www.DarrenSugiyama.com

Copyright © 2024 Darren Sugiyama
ISBN: 078-1-312-06243-6

DARREN SUGIYAMA

Table Of Contents

Chapter 1: Premium Financing In 2024…………………. pg. 7

Chapter 2: Understanding The Concept…………………. pg. 11

Chapter 3: The Tax-Free Benefits Of Life Insurance…... pg. 19

Chapter 4: How IUL Policy Charges Actually Work....... pg. 25

Chapter 5: How IUL Floors & Caps Work...................... pg. 31

Chapter 6: How Policy Drawdowns Work……………... pg. 39

Chapter 7: Are IUL Multiplier Bonuses Too Risky?....... pg. 45

Chapter 8: Why Backtesting Is So Important…............. pg. 49

Chapter 9: Estate Planning Using PFLI…….....……… pg. 61

Chapter 10: First-Dollar Financing………………....……. pg. 71

Chapter 11: Second-Year Financing (2YF)………………. pg. 87

Chapter 12: Partial-Equity Interest Accrual (PEIA)…….. pg. 91

Chapter 13: Third-Year Financing (3YF)………………... pg. 97

Chapter 14: Sixth-Year Financing (6YF)………………... pg. 105

Chapter 15: The Myth Of Free Life Insurance………….. pg. 113

Chapter 16: The Sin Of Miscalculating Collateral………. pg. 121

Chapter 17: High Interest Rates & Recessions………….. pg. 125

Chapter 18: Should PFLI Be Used For Retirement?.......... pg. 129

Chapter 19: Gimmicks To Avoid………………………... pg. 135

Chapter 20: The History Of The Author………………... pg. 141

DARREN SUGIYAMA

Disclaimer:

The author of this book is not a CPA or tax attorney. Nothing in this book shall be misconstrued as tax advice or legal advice. For any tax-related or legal-related questions or concerns, it is highly recommended that you consult your CPA, tax professional, or tax attorney regarding these specific topics.

Chapter 1
Premium Financing In 2024

Each year, *Esquire* magazine releases a special issue they call *The Big Black Book.* It is a style manual for men with a discerning eye – connoisseurs of the best luxury products and experiences life has to offer a man with financial means – and it is updated annually. It reviews the newest cutting edge *James Bondesque* gadgets, must-have wardrobe additions, the sexiest newly released Italian sports cars, and the hottest exotic travel destinations. It encompasses everything an *International Man Of Mystery* ought to know about what is *new & hot* each year.

As I recently thought about *Esquire's The Big Black Book* concept, it made me consider updating a book that I originally wrote back in 2021: *Premium Financed Life Insurance - The Key To Effect Estate Tax Planning.*

With all the changes this industry has undergone in recent years (months even), I have come to realize that in order for any book on this subject matter to be accurate, relevant, and truly educational, it must be updated annually.

I figured if I am going to continue to call myself *The Most Transparent Premium Financing Intermediary In The Life Insurance Industry*, then I had better live up to it, consistently putting out *new/updated/relevant* content, keeping me on the cutting edge of this industry. That's what a true leader does.

I always say, *"The better you get, the better you better get."*

Many irresponsibly designed premium financing cases – wherein the client either has an absurdly small amount of *skin-in-the-game* (and in some cases, no financial contributions whatsoever) – are now imploding due to the accelerated compound debt that has come as a result of increased borrowing rates. In these types of premium financing arrangements, *Loan-To-Value (LTV)* ratios have become less and less healthy, causing clients to post substantially more collateral than they originally expected. The harsh reality is, many of these clients were not truly made aware of the consequence of increasing interest rates, making the entire model unsuitable for certain types of clients.

As an example of just how much borrowing interest rates have increased over the last couple of years, see below:

30-Day Average SOFR	1-Year CMT
01/03/2022: 0.05%	01/04/2022: 0.38%
01/03/2023: 4.12%	01/03/2023: 4.72%
11/03/2023: 5.32%	11/03/2023: 5.37%

To see today's *30-Day Average SOFR* rates, go to *https://fred.stlouisfed.org/series/SOFR30DAYAVG*, and for *1-Year CMT* rates, go to *https://fred.stlouisfed.org/series/DGS1*.

For clients paying interest out-of-pocket, these increased interest rates now require a substantially larger client outlay. For clients that made their decision to enter a premium financing arrangement based on accruing the interest, their debt is compounding at an extremely accelerated rate, potentially outpacing the policy's cash value growth. If this happens, their *Loan-To-Value (LTV)* ratio becomes extremely vulnerable to either huge collateral calls (during the time while there is a third-party lender involved), or a policy lapse (after the third-party lender is paid off using a *policy withdrawal* or *policy loan*).

It has been my experience that most clients that purchased *Premium Financed Life Insurance* from these overly aggressive intermediary firms were never truly educated on these types of potential risk factors. This lack of full disclosure and lack of transparency on behalf of the *Premium Financing Intermediary* is what has given the life insurance industry a bad name.

Conversely, I have built my reputation in this industry as a *conservative and transparent educator*, not an *insurance salesman*. I have found that with uber high net worth clients, my approach to *premium financing* – which is rooted in education and consumer protection – has been a breath of fresh air for them.

Most life insurance agents gloss over the details, and they justify this lack of disclosure and lack of transparency with their mantra "K.I.S.S. – *Keep It Simple Stupid.*"

My response to hearing this irresponsible justification is, *"There is nothing SIMPLE about Premium Financed Life Insurance, STUPID."*

If done properly – with the proper due diligence, stress-testing, and backtesting – *Premium Financed Life Insurance* is an extremely prudent and efficient tool when it comes to estate planning. Dumbing down the sophistication of this strategy negates the mathematical validity of using *responsible leverage*, which is why I have committed myself to being an educator and a nationally renowned author on this particular topic in an industry that is severely lacking in this area.

This is the eleventh book I have authored in my career. Several of my books are currently being distributed in multiple countries including Australia, Brasil, Canada, Croatia, Czechoslovakia, Denmark, India, Italy, Japan, Mexico, New Zealand, Norway, Singapore, Sweden, the United Kingdom, and of course, the United States of America.

If you are reading this book, my guess is that you are either a financial professional that is considering introducing the concept of *Premium Financed Life Insurance* to your clients, or you are an individual who is considering using *Premium Financed Life Insurance* as a wealth preservation strategy for yourself and your family.

Premium Financed Life Insurance is not appropriate for everybody. However for the *right* client – assuming they have the right net worth, understand the power of leverage, and have the intellectual capacity to make sound mathematical decisions – it can be one of the most valuable components in their overall financial portfolio.

If you are a financial advisor, life insurance agent, CPA, estate planning attorney, or a principal in a family office, this book seeks to give you a better understanding of my premium financing methodology, risk analysis process, policy design artistry, and suitability study analysis. This level of full transparency is something that is not only important in premium financing, but it is a pillar of how I do business, as well as how I live my life as a husband, father, Christian, and as a man of Samurai decent.

The new content I will be covering in this *Updated 2024 Edition* will include some of the radical changes that have happened in this industry within the last few years, as well as some new strategies and offerings I have designed for the advisor community.

I will provide answers to these questions:

1. Does premium financing work in a high interest rate environment?
2. How do you explain the low index crediting rates in carrier illustrations?
3. How are you dealing with clients that are upset that the combination of high interest rates and low index crediting illustrations are depicting an unfavorable outcome?
4. What is the future of borrowing interest rates?
5. Why do clients seem to always get higher-than-expected collateral calls?
6. Why is it important to have multiple loan models and lending platform designs for different types of clients?

I will bluntly and transparently answer these FAQs, as well as address some of the most important issues when a client is considering *Premium Financed Life Insurance* as a component of their estate plan.

I once heard the head of a large life insurance distribution channel – while speaking to a financial advisor – say, *"Sugiyama won't even sugarcoat a cookie."*

This is absolutely true.

I do my best to communicate respectfully, however I believe in telling everyone the truth about the *good, bad, and ugly* components of *Premium Financed Life Insurance*.

I truly hope you find value in this book.

Chapter 2
Understanding The Concept

My name is Darren Sugiyama and I am a *Premium Financing Intermediary*, which means I specialize in working with financial professionals all over the country that rely on me to do one thing and one thing only: <u>To design the most mathematically prudent method of financing their clients' life insurance premiums</u>.

When an individual's net worth reaches a certain level, it often times makes sense for them to purchase their life insurance policy using a third-party lender's capital instead of using their own capital. Although premium financing may seem like a foreign concept you, chances are, you have probably already purchased some of your other valuable assets using *leverage*. Perhaps you purchased your home using a mortgage loan, or financed the purchase of your automobiles, or expanded your business with a line of credit. When it comes to purchasing life insurance, the concept of using *leverage* is not so different.

Using the analogy of purchasing real estate with a mortgage loan is not a perfectly symmetrical analogy to *Premium Financed Life Insurance*, but it is close, and it is a good way to help those new to the concept to understand the general idea.

In an attempt to articulate this general concept, I will compare the purchase of a $10,000,000 property using a *"mortgage loan"* to the cash purchase of a $3,850,000 property. The reason I am using quotations in calling this a *"mortgage loan"* is that in this analogous model, I am structuring the *"mortgage loan"* to emulate a *Premium Financed Life Insurance* loan structure (not a conventional mortgage loan structure).

Assuming the $10,000,000 property was purchased by borrowing $1,000,000 per year from the lender over the course of ten years, the buyer would pay the interest due (interest-only payments) on the cumulative loan balance each year. At a borrowing rate of 7.00%, over a 10-year period, the buyer would have paid $3,850,000 in total interest payments.

YEAR	BORROW ANNUALLY	CUMULATIVE LOAN BAL	INTEREST RATE	ANNUAL INTEREST PAYMENTS
1	$1,000,000	$1,000,000	7.00%	$70,000
2	$1,000,000	$2,000,000	7.00%	$140,000
3	$1,000,000	$3,000,000	7.00%	$210,000
4	$1,000,000	$4,000,000	7.00%	$280,000
5	$1,000,000	$5,000,000	7.00%	$350,000
6	$1,000,000	$6,000,000	7.00%	$420,000
7	$1,000,000	$7,000,000	7.00%	$490,000
8	$1,000,000	$8,000,000	7.00%	$560,000
9	$1,000,000	$9,000,000	7.00%	$630,000
10	$1,000,000	$10,000,000	7.00%	$700,000
				$3,850,000

If the initial $10,000,000 property value appreciated at a rate of 7.00% per year, the gross value would become $19,671,514 by the end of the tenth year. But remember, there would still be $10,000,000 of debt owed to the lender due to the buyer making interest-only payments (not paying down any principal yet). After backing out the debt, the net value of the property would be $9,671,514 ($19,671,514 minus $10,000,000 equals $9,671,514).

YEAR	INITIAL PROPERTY VALUE	ANNUAL APPRECIATION	EOY PROPERTY VALUE
1	$10,000,000	7.00%	$10,700,000
2		7.00%	$11,449,000
3		7.00%	$12,250,430
4		7.00%	$13,107,960
5		7.00%	$14,025,517
6		7.00%	$15,007,304
7		7.00%	$16,057,815
8		7.00%	$17,181,862
9		7.00%	$18,384,592
10		7.00%	$19,671,514
		Mortgage Debt:	-$10,000,000
		Net Value:	**$9,671,514**

Alternatively, the buyer could just purchase a $3,850,000 property with cash (no leverage). Below is the same payment schedule as the previous example, however the payments are being applied to the $3,850,000 purchase price (non-financed). The purpose of this scenario is to illustrate the buying power of leverage in the previous example in an apples-to-apples comparison.

YEAR	ANNUAL CASH PAYMENTS
1	$70,000
2	$140,000
3	$210,000
4	$280,000
5	$350,000
6	$420,000
7	$490,000
8	$560,000
9	$630,000
10	$700,000
	$3,850,000

If the initial $3,850,000 property value appreciated at the same rate of 7.00% per year, the gross value would become $7,573,533 at the end of the tenth year. There would be no debt on this purchase since it was a cash purchase. Compared to the $9,671,514 net value of the financed property in the previous example, the non-financed property net value would have a $2,097,981 lesser net value (21.69% less).

YEAR	INITIAL PROPERTY VALUE	ANNUAL APPRECIATION	EOY PROPERTY VALUE
1	$3,850,000	7.00%	$4,119,500
2		7.00%	$4,407,865
3		7.00%	$4,716,416
4		7.00%	$5,046,565
5		7.00%	$5,399,824
6		7.00%	$5,777,812
7		7.00%	$6,182,259
8		7.00%	$6,615,017
9		7.00%	$7,078,068
10		7.00%	$7,573,533
		Mortgage Debt:	$0
		Non-Financed Property Net Value:	$7,573,533
		vs.	vs.
		Financed Property Net Value:	$9,671,514
		Greater Net Value of Financed Property:	**$2,097,981**

Though this analogy is not an exact parallel to *Premium Financed Life Insurance*, it is a good way to understand the concept from a philosophical perspective.

Using a real-world example, below is an actual *Premium Financing* design wherein the client pays interest-only (column 1) and takes drawdowns from the policy value to recover 100% of the client's interest expense that was paid in years 1-10, producing a net zero cost. The death benefit stays above $10,000,000 throughout the life of the policy all the way until age 120 (though the ledger below only shows a 40-year window up until age 94).

PREMIUM FINANCING
(WITH 100% COST RECOVERY)

YR	AGE	1 CLIENT CONTRIBUTION	2 COST RECOVERY DRAWDOWNS	3 CASH VALUE NET OF LOANS	4 DEATH BENEFIT NET OF LOANS
1	55	-$178,000	$0	$0	$36,276,601
2	56	-$360,990	$0	$0	$36,177,261
3	57	-$549,130	$0	$0	$36,187,564
4	58	-$742,589	$0	$0	$36,327,656
5	59	-$941,536	$0	$0	$36,619,029
6	60	-$1,146,148	$0	$0	$37,072,539
7	61	-$1,356,605	$0	$675,374	$37,698,013
8	62	-$1,376,458	$0	$1,610,347	$38,567,781
9	63	-$1,396,740	$0	$2,591,272	$39,483,501
10	64	-$1,417,459	$0	$3,687,323	$40,449,143
11	65	$0	$0	$3,996,188	$17,248,124
12	66	$0	$0	$4,174,625	$17,398,933
13	67	$0	$0	$4,363,683	$17,549,443
14	68	$0	$0	$4,561,381	$17,694,620
15	69	$0	$0	$4,767,375	$17,832,720
16	70	$0	$0	$5,113,695	$17,827,193
17	71	$0	$0	$5,476,113	$17,787,154
18	72	$0	$0	$5,854,529	$17,708,430
19	73	$0	$0	$6,257,776	$17,596,197
20	74	$0	$0	$6,688,325	$17,448,024
21	75	$0	$0	$7,149,199	$18,003,206
22	76	$0	$0	$7,633,526	$18,586,577
23	77	$0	$0	$8,275,108	$10,338,806
24	78	$0	$0	$8,960,908	$11,141,394
25	79	$0	$0	$9,692,832	$11,996,536
26	80	$0	$631,044	$9,803,726	$12,237,057
27	81	$0	$631,044	$9,920,723	$12,490,191
28	82	$0	$631,044	$10,041,291	$12,753,590
29	83	$0	$631,044	$10,162,178	$13,024,162
30	84	$0	$631,044	$10,277,912	$13,296,506
31	85	$0	$631,044	$10,380,702	$13,562,801
32	86	$0	$631,044	$10,460,624	$13,813,001
33	87	$0	$631,044	$10,504,253	$14,033,409
34	88	$0	$631,044	$10,502,030	$14,214,401
35	89	$0	$631,044	$10,436,027	$14,337,592
36	90	$0	$631,044	$10,282,863	$13,559,683
37	91	$0	$631,044	$10,152,774	$12,733,821
38	92	$0	$631,044	$10,082,046	$11,890,463
39	93	$0	$631,044	$10,124,603	$11,076,033
40	94	$0	$631,044	$10,349,975	$10,349,974
		-$9,465,655 TOTAL INTEREST PAID	$9,465,655 COST RECOVERY		

$0 NET COST

Alternatively, the client could just purchase a *Non-Financed Life Insurance Policy* with a $10,000,016 level death benefit. The annual premium would be $233,330 for a period of fifteen years.

Though the client's annual payments would be less in years 2-10 (compared to the *Premium Financed* arrangement), there would be no cost recovery drawdowns from the policy value, resulting in a $3,499,950 net cost (compared to the zero net cost of the *Premium Financing* arrangement). In addition, there would be substantially more net death benefit in the financed arrangement throughout the life of the policy.

NON-FINANCED IUL
(NO COST RECOVERY)

YR	AGE	1 CLIENT CONTRIBUTION	2 COST RECOVERY DRAWDOWNS	3 NET CASH VALUE	4 DEATH BENEFIT NET OF LOANS
1	55	-$233,330	$0	$0	$10,000,016
2	56	-$233,330	$0	$39,571	$10,000,016
3	57	-$233,330	$0	$242,697	$10,000,016
4	58	-$233,330	$0	$451,604	$10,000,016
5	59	-$233,330	$0	$670,283	$10,000,016
6	60	-$233,330	$0	$899,854	$10,000,016
7	61	-$233,330	$0	$1,141,081	$10,000,016
8	62	-$233,330	$0	$1,394,762	$10,000,016
9	63	-$233,330	$0	$1,661,518	$10,000,016
10	64	-$233,330	$0	$1,966,234	$10,000,016
11	65	-$233,330	$0	$2,293,377	$10,000,016
12	66	-$233,330	$0	$2,635,499	$10,000,016
13	67	-$233,330	$0	$2,946,177	$10,000,016
14	68	-$233,330	$0	$3,272,078	$10,000,016
15	69	-$233,330	$0	$3,613,980	$10,000,016
16	70	$0	$0	$3,788,294	$10,000,016
17	71	$0	$0	$3,966,846	$10,000,016
18	72	$0	$0	$4,148,986	$10,000,016
19	73	$0	$0	$4,338,291	$10,000,016
20	74	$0	$0	$4,535,094	$10,000,016
21	75	$0	$0	$4,739,818	$10,000,016
22	76	$0	$0	$4,952,825	$10,000,016
23	77	$0	$0	$5,174,825	$10,000,016
24	78	$0	$0	$5,402,242	$10,000,016
25	79	$0	$0	$5,634,903	$10,000,016
26	80	$0	$0	$5,872,310	$10,000,016
27	81	$0	$0	$6,110,221	$10,000,016
28	82	$0	$0	$6,347,515	$10,000,016
29	83	$0	$0	$6,583,395	$10,000,016
30	84	$0	$0	$6,815,733	$10,000,016
31	85	$0	$0	$7,041,783	$10,000,016
32	86	$0	$0	$7,258,950	$10,000,016
33	87	$0	$0	$7,463,900	$10,000,016
34	88	$0	$0	$7,658,670	$10,000,016
35	89	$0	$0	$7,840,774	$10,000,016
36	90	$0	$0	$8,006,577	$10,000,016
37	91	$0	$0	$8,156,470	$10,000,016
38	92	$0	$0	$8,287,951	$10,000,016
39	93	$0	$0	$8,400,657	$10,000,016
40	94	$0	$0	$8,494,690	$10,000,016
		-$3,499,950 TOTAL CLIENT OUTLAY			

-$3,499,950 NET COST

The other logical alternative would be to invest the same client outlay of the *Premium Financed* arrangement into a *Non-Insurance Based Investment Account*.

In this arrangement, I am assuming the same *cost recovery* drawdowns as the *Premium Financed* arrangement. I am also assuming a 38.10% Capital Gains Tax Rate, an all-in investment fee of 1.35%, and an estate tax rate of 40.00%. By not incorporating *Premium Financed Life Insurance* in this portfolio, we see a substantially less favorable outcome below.

INVESTMENT ACCOUNT
(WITH 100% COST RECOVERY)

YR	AGE	1 CLIENT CONTRIBUTION	2 COST RECOVERY DRAWDOWNS	3 PRE-ESTATE TAX VALUE	4 INHERITED BY G2 AFTER 40% ESTATE TAXES
1	55	-$178,000	$0	$183,123	$109,874
2	56	-$360,990	$0	$559,775	$335,865
3	57	-$549,130	$0	$1,140,823	$684,494
4	58	-$742,589	$0	$1,937,623	$1,162,574
5	59	-$941,536	$0	$2,962,032	$1,777,219
6	60	-$1,146,148	$0	$4,226,427	$2,535,856
7	61	-$1,356,605	$0	$5,743,732	$3,446,239
8	62	-$1,376,458	$0	$7,325,134	$4,395,080
9	63	-$1,396,740	$0	$8,972,920	$5,383,752
10	64	-$1,417,459	$0	$10,689,450	$6,413,670
11	65	$0	$0	$10,997,130	$6,598,278
12	66	$0	$0	$11,313,666	$6,788,200
13	67	$0	$0	$11,639,313	$6,983,588
14	68	$0	$0	$11,974,333	$7,184,600
15	69	$0	$0	$12,318,996	$7,391,398
16	70	$0	$0	$12,673,580	$7,604,148
17	71	$0	$0	$13,038,370	$7,823,022
18	72	$0	$0	$13,413,660	$8,048,196
19	73	$0	$0	$13,799,752	$8,279,851
20	74	$0	$0	$14,196,957	$8,518,174
21	75	$0	$0	$14,605,595	$8,763,357
22	76	$0	$0	$15,025,995	$9,015,597
23	77	$0	$0	$15,458,496	$9,275,098
24	78	$0	$0	$15,903,446	$9,542,068
25	79	$0	$0	$16,361,203	$9,816,722
26	80	$0	$631,044	$16,182,928	$9,709,757
27	81	$0	$631,044	$15,999,522	$9,599,713
28	82	$0	$631,044	$15,810,837	$9,486,502
29	83	$0	$631,044	$15,616,721	$9,370,032
30	84	$0	$631,044	$15,417,017	$9,250,210
31	85	$0	$631,044	$15,211,566	$9,126,939
32	86	$0	$631,044	$15,000,201	$9,000,120
33	87	$0	$631,044	$14,782,752	$8,869,651
34	88	$0	$631,044	$14,559,044	$8,735,426
35	89	$0	$631,044	$14,328,896	$8,597,338
36	90	$0	$631,044	$14,092,125	$8,455,275
37	91	$0	$631,044	$13,848,538	$8,309,123
38	92	$0	$631,044	$13,597,940	$8,158,764
39	93	$0	$631,044	$13,340,129	$8,004,078
40	94	$0	$631,044	$13,074,898	$7,844,939
		-$9,465,655 TOTAL CLIENT OUTLAY	$9,465,655 COST RECOVERY		

$0
NET COST

To illustrate a comparison of outcomes between the three strategies just discussed, the line graph below illustrates an extremely compelling argument in favor of *Premium Financed Life Insurance* using the data from the previous pages.

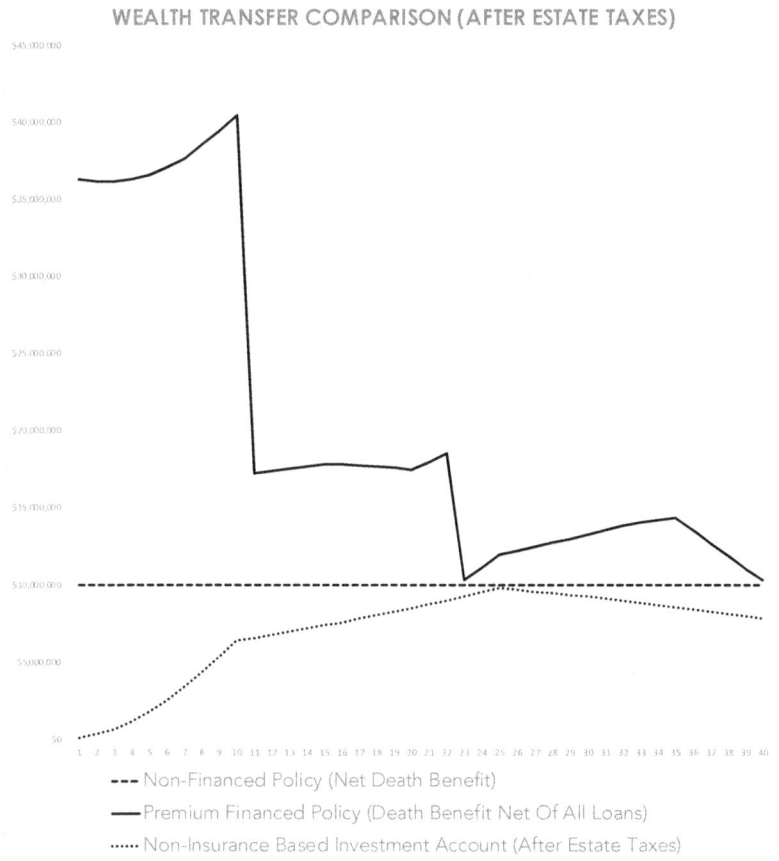

What makes this even more compelling is the fact that in the *Premium Financed Life Insurance* depiction, I used third-party borrowing interest rates that started at 7.12% in year one and increased them 100bps by the tenth year (8.12%). At the time of illustrating this comparison (November 2023), the *Forward Curve Rate* was projected to only be 6.80% by the tenth year instead of the 8.12% rate I modeled. To see the *Forward Curve Rates* go to: *https://www.chathamfinancial.com/technology/us-forward-curves*

This is just one of many examples of how conservative I am in designing my financing models.

Additionally, I illustrated the policy index return assumption at only 6.00%, making the borrowing rate perpetually higher than the index crediting rate in all years (214bps higher in year ten), causing a substantial negative arbitrage percentage-wise.

While most other *Premium Financing Intermediaries* (my so-called competitors) drop the borrowing rate after a few years to make their proposition look more appealing, I design my proposals depicting an ever-increasing borrowing rate. Though this is not what the *Forward Curve Rates* expect in the future, I think it is important to show the client what outcomes might look like if borrowing rates do not decrease in the way the *Forward Curve Rates* project.

It is my brand to under-promise in order to increase the chances of over-delivering and exceeding my original conservative depictions. From a educational and consumer protection perspective, I believe this is the prudent, most transparent, and most honorable way to communicate potential outcomes to clients. If the premium financing design is mathematically prudent and can withstand market volatility, a poor sequence of index returns, and less-than-ideal cash value performance, I believe using these environments as the benchmark to make wise client decisions reinforces my duty as a fiduciarily responsible advisor. In my opinion, to do otherwise dishonors this duty.

Hopefully this chapter has laid down a base foundation of understanding regarding the concept of *Premium Financed Life Insurance*.

Now it is time to go deep down the rabbit hole to give you a thorough, highly-detailed, granular understanding of all the moving parts, not solely regarding the financing aspect, but also the components of the actual product – the *Indexed Universal Life Insurance* policy design.

In this book, I will discuss *why* it works, *when* it works, when it does *not work*, and most importantly, who should *not* employ this strategy.

Chapter 3
The Tax-Free Benefits Of Life Insurance

The three most common uses of life insurance are to:
1. Provide liquidity to fund lifestyle expenses for one's family in the event of a pre-mature death.
2. Generate a tax-free supplemental retirement income.
3. Pay the estate taxes due when wealth is transferred to the next generation.

The tax-advantaged treatment of the cash value accumulation inside a life insurance policy is very appealing for those who want a conservative alternative to a *taxable stocks and bonds portfolio*. This tax-free benefit can also be enjoyed when taking tax-free retirement income drawdowns from the policy. I have an entire chapter in this book devoted to explaining the different ways to take these tax-free income drawdowns.

In addition, when a wealthy individual passes away, their assets can be passed on to their surviving spouse without tax consequence, however once their surviving spouse passes away and their wealth is transferred to the next generation, their heirs can incur a substantial tax liability in the form of *estate taxes*. The IRS allows a certain amount of their net worth to be transferred to the next generation tax-free up until a certain dollar amount known as the *Estate Tax Exemption Limit*. In 2017, the *Trump Tax Act* was enacted, giving individuals an $11,180,000 estate tax exemption starting in 2018 (up from $5,490,000 in 2017). This exemption has increased each year since then. Below, we see these increases since 2017 (sourced from *https://www.irs.gov/pub/irs-pdf/i706.pdf*):

2017: $5,490,000 ($10,980,000 per married couple)
2018: $11,180,000 ($22,360,000 per married couple)
2019: $11,400,000 ($22,800,000 per married couple)
2020: $11,580,000 ($23,160,000 per married couple)
2021: $11,700,000 ($23,400,000 per married couple)
2022: $12,060,000 ($24,120,000 per married couple)
2023: $12,920,000 ($25,840,000 per married couple)

Upon death, a spouse can pass their exemption on to their surviving spouse. However what many feared regarding the *Biden Administration's* tax agenda came to pass on September 13, 2021 when the *House Ways and Means Committee* released a tax change proposal in favor of reducing the estate tax exemption limit back down to the $5,000,000 range per individual in 2026.

However, one thing that has remained constant is the favorable tax treatment of life insurance, which is why it continues to be an incredibly valuable estate planning tool.

Due to *Section 101a* of the IRS tax code, the death benefit of a life insurance policy is tax-free, giving policy owners a huge advantage when the policy is owned in an *Irrevocable Life Insurance Trust (ILIT)* outside their taxable estate. I will discuss comparing life insurance strategies to non-insurance-based alternatives later in this book, however it is important to understand that when a person dies, any excess net worth above the estate tax exemption is currently taxed at a rate of 40.00% when it is transferred to the next generation.

To clarify how this works, when one spouse passes away, the surviving spouse does not incur any estate tax liability. However when the second spouse dies and the estate is transferred to the next generation, estate taxes are incurred by the inheriting generation.

As an example, if the surviving spouse is worth $100,000,000 above the exemption limit, the inheriting generation will owe $40,000,000 in estate taxes (40.00% of the $100,000,000). This inheriting generation is only given nine months from the time of their surviving parent's death to file and pay the estate taxes due, which is not much lead time by any means.

Even if the estate value is comprised of illiquid assets (e.g., real estate, a company, jewelry, art, automobile collection, etc.), the estate tax is still due on the value of these assets nonetheless, which often results in a necessary *fire sale* of such assets to come up with the funds required to pay the estate taxes. This can be both financially draining and emotionally taxing for all parties involved.

Life insurance is an extremely efficient tool in planning for the estate tax liability that the next generation will incur because it removes the need to liquidate the estate's illiquid assets within this nine-month period. If the policy is owned by an *Irrevocable Life Insurance Trust (ILIT)* – which is outside the taxable estate – the death benefit will pay out tax-free to the *ILIT* and is not subject to estate taxes. The *ILIT* can then pay the estate taxes due once the death benefit is issued. This is a much easier process to manage than a desperate *fire sale* of illiquid assets just to come up with the cash needed to pay the estate taxes.

There are many benefits of using life insurance as both an estate tax planning tool, as well as a tax-advantaged asset for wealth accumulation and supplemental retirement income. But this is an industry wherein the explanations of how these insurance-based instruments actually work is *opaque* at best. One of the biggest criticisms of the life insurance industry is that many of the products lack transparency, and quite frankly, I would have to agree with that accusation... sort of, but not completely.

The reality is that many of these life insurance products do not lack transparency in their *construction*. The lack of transparency is in how their construction is *communicated* to the client – both from the carriers and the agents. It is a problem I experienced as a life insurance *client* back before I got into this line of work, and it is a problem that still exists today. To make things even worse, when the concept of premium financing is introduced into an already-opaque equation, the complexities, perceived risk, confusion, and skepticism grow exponentially.

That being said, I have the solution to these seemingly daunting issues and accusations which I will articulate in this book.

The key is to understand how different types of life insurance policies are built and how they work mechanically. This is the foundation I built my practice on. Everything I do is rooted in education and granular understanding.

In this book, I will open up the *black box* so you can see what's actually inside the box, which will change your perspective from looking through *opaque lenses* to looking through a *high-powered microscope*. The strong stance I have taken on opening up this *black box* has at times felt like I was opening *Pandora's Box*, but as I stated earlier, I am an industry disruptor – a beacon of transparency – and my goal is to teach you the truth about these products, where the risks are, how to mitigate these risks, and to show you the best way to utilize these products in the most effective way possible.

If you are not familiar with the details of the Greek mythological story of *Pandora's Box*, indulge me for just a moment to share with you how analogous this story is to *Premium Financed Life Insurance*.

In Greek mythology, *Pandora* was the first woman on Earth. She was given a box that the gods told her contained special gifts, but she was also told that she was not allowed to open it and see what was inside.

Eventually, *Pandora* could not contain her curiosity and she opened the box. When she did, all the illnesses and hardships that the gods had hidden in the box started coming out. She tried to close the box once she saw the evil coming out of it, but in doing so, *hope* got trapped inside the box.

Many people feel the same way about certain life insurance products. They are told that the *black box* contains all kinds of special gifts (e.g., tax-free benefits, 0% floor, etc.), but they are told not to open the box and dissect its components at the granular level. In fact, I've even heard advisors say, *"My clients don't want to know all the details."*

Personally, I think that statement greatly underestimates the curiosity of high-net worth clients. To say that a person worth $100 million doesn't want to understand how an *IUL* works is an incredibly naïve thing to say, and from my own personal experience, a very inaccurate thing to say.

My method of communicating the construction of a *Premium Financed Life Insurance* arrangement is to break down my explanation into following chronological sections:

    1. The different purposes of life insurance within estate planning.

2. The concept of using leverage in the form of financing some or all of the premiums.

3. My backtesting and stress-testing methodology.

4. How interest rates and policy performance can impact the amount of collateral required.

5. How policy charges work.

6. How policy crediting works.

7. How a poor sequence of market returns can impact both short-term and long-term outcomes.

8. The history of the relationship between market performance and borrowing interest rates.

9. A comparison between premium financed life insurance versus a non-financed policy, versus a non-insurance based investment account after fees, capital gains tax, and estate tax.

Before I transition from section to section, I always tell the client, *"I tend to get extremely detailed because I'm a math nerd, so if at any time I start getting too granular, just tell me you don't need to know that much detail, and I'll stay more conceptual and not get so granular."*

Guess how many times a client has told me to *not* explain the details to them. Not once. Ever.

When I started teaching advisors and their clients how *Premium Financed IULs* work at the granular level, my result was much different than *Pandora's* because when I opened up the *black box* of *IULs*, not only did the evils of the life insurance industry come out, but so did *hope*. Sure, I exposed certain products and their design flaws (especially in premium financing), but I have also been able to uncover the truth about how a well-designed *Premium Financed IUL* can be one of the most valuable assets in estate planning that exists – assuming it is designed properly and used with the right client.

As I mentioned earlier this book, before I knew anything about life insurance, my financial advisor lost me $930,000 in three years due to a poorly designed life insurance strategy. I'm still not certain whether or not he was aware of what he was doing when he designed that strategy.

If he was *aware*, he was commission-greedy and unethical.

If he was *unaware*, then he was irresponsible and incompetent.

Either way, I was the one got hurt financially.

The purpose of this book is to teach you how these products actually work – specifically the *Indexed Universal Life Insurance (IUL)* product – so that you fully understand not only the general concept, but the granular details as well.

I will also teach you several different ways to finance life insurance premiums because each specific financing arrangement should be custom designed for each specific client.

In this book, I will dive into a thorough explanation of how life insurance can be utilized in effective estate tax planning, but before I delve into its application, I will first explain how the *IUL* product is constructed, beginning with what most believe to be a black box – *policy charges*.

Chapter 4
How IUL Policy Charges Actually Work

When most financial professionals measure risk, they typically have conversations about *Standard Deviation*, *Sharpe Ratios*, and *Monte Carlo* simulations.

These risk-measuring techniques are certainly important topics of discussion because they address the *Probability Of Risk*, however they all fail to articulate the most important element of risk: *The Consequence Of Risk*.

I was once asked if my proprietary backtesting software ran *Monte Carlo* simulations. I understood the spirit of their question, however I explained that *Monte Carlo* simulations merely measure the *Probability Of Risk*. So I asked him what level of risk he was comfortable with. 80% probability of a positive outcome? 90% probability of a positive outcome?

The gentleman told me he was comfortable with a 90% probability of a positive outcome (10% probability of a negative outcome).

I said, *"Okay, if I put ten hand guns on the table, and NINE of them have no bullets in them, but ONE of the ten has a bullet in the chamber, how comfortable are you picking up one of the guns, putting it to your head, and squeezing the trigger?"*

His comfort level with 90% probability of a positive outcome quickly faded. In this scenario, the *Probability Of Risk* was relatively low, however the *Consequence Of Risk* was extremely high.

In premium financing, I focus on modeling what happens in a scenario where a severely negative set of circumstances occurs, even if the probability is only 1%. Though I am concerned about the *Probability Of Risk*, I am far more concerned with *The Consequence Of Risk*.

The *Consequence Of Risk* in premium financing is severe – a lapsing policy – which can happen if the compounding debt of interest accrual outpaces the policy value's growth. However the risk of interest accrual is not solely limited to the third-party loan debt balance. Its liability also exists in the debt accrual that occurs in a *Participating Loan* with the carrier (which I will discuss at great length later in this book). If the cash value growth (due to the index credit) does not outpace the policy charges and the internal accrued interest debt, the net value of the policy may erode, potentially resulting in an early policy lapse. The probability of this happening drastically increases when a premium financing arrangement is too aggressively designed wherein the client does not have enough *skin-in-the-game*.

The *Probability Of Risk* in an over-leveraged, overly-aggressive premium financing arrangement is too high for most clients' financial strength and risk tolerance levels. I provide the *premium financing seatbelt* (reducing the *Probability Of Risk*), as well as the simulated crash test results (modeling the *Consequence Of Risk)* in order to evaluate whether or not premium financing is appropriate for the client.

Sure, there are extremely rare exceptions where *high-risk tolerant* clients choose to employ hyper-aggressive leverage-on-leverage tactics, but for the most part, life insurance should be a conservative piece of a client's overall financial portfolio, especially when it comes to estate tax planning. I specialize in the conservative approach to premium financing.

Though I am not a CPA or tax attorney (which means that I cannot give tax advice or legal advice), I can mathematically model different premium financing strategies, compare them to non-insurance-based solutions, and showcase different financial outcomes using certain tax assumptions. I can also model certain unfavorable assumptions that put extra strains on the premium financed solutions, which I think is vitally important to model for clients in the spirit of full transparency and proper due diligence.

This industry lacks full client disclosure, so being the *beacon of transparency* – albeit a self-proclaimed title – is the main reason I am the trusted source of premium financing for top advisors, producer groups, CPAs, tax attorneys, family offices, and carriers in the life insurance industry.

If the spirit of advisor/client conversations is rooted in education, consumer protection, and risk mitigation, then the foundation of these conversations will be client-centric, which is what they should be. My goal in all communication efforts is to transparently articulate how the math works, and if the indisputable math tells us that one particular method of premium financing is the most advantageous to the client compared to other viable alternatives in an array of backtested scenarios (I analyze 121 different historical 40-year periods), the decision to move forward with that particular design is an obvious one. I have devoted an entire chapter to explaining how my backtesting software works.

Conversely, there have even been scenarios where my mathematical modeling process proved that it was *not* in the client's best interest to finance their life insurance premiums, and in such scenarios, I am the first one to discourage them from using premium financing as a strategy. Some advisors don't like that I'm so blunt with my recommendations against premium financing in these scenarios, and some of them will even try to get me to rework the numbers to favor the premium financing proposition. In these rare instances, my answer is always the same: *The math either works, or it doesn't work. The math doesn't lie.*

Remember, I'm the guy that won't even sugarcoat a cookie.

Your journey in understanding the true *Consequence Of Risk* in poorly designed *Premium Financed IUL* policies starts with understanding how policy charges and credits actually work.

When a carrier receives the policy premium for an *IUL* product, the first charge that is deducted is the *Premium Load*. Assuming the premium is paid annually at the *Beginning Of The Year (BOY)*, the *Premium Loads* are also deducted at the *BOY*. The remaining policy charges (e.g., Cost of Insurance, Administration Fees, Mortality Expenses, etc.) are then deducted monthly.

Assuming the client selected a *1-Year Annual Point-To-Point* index option, the *segment* begins in the month the premium is swept into the index account (e.g., the 15th day of the month), and ends twelve months later. At the end of this 12-month segment, the index credit is then determined based on the underlying index's performance during that 1-year segment wherein the *IUL's* cap and floor would be applied to the gross accumulated value of the policy (not the *net* cash surrender value, but the *gross* accumulated value). Some carriers apply this index credit to the *EOY Accumulated Value (EOYAV)*, whereas other carriers apply the index return to the *Average Monthly Accumulated Value (AMAV)*.

Mathematically speaking, the *AMAV* is a higher number than the *EOYAV* because it does not account for 100% of the monthly charges. In other words, in the second month of the segment, only 2/12 of the monthly charges have been deducted, hence the accumulated value in that month would be higher than the accumulated value in the eleventh month wherein 11/12 of the monthly charges were deducted.

For the sake of this discussion, we will assume that the *Indexed Universal Life (IUL)* insurance product applies the index credit to the *EOY Accumulated Value*. We will also assume that the product's underlying index tracks the S&P 500's performance, with a 0.00% floor and a 9.00% cap. In the event that the S&P 500 produced a positive return of 15.00% in a given year, the policy index credit would credit 9.00%, not exceeding the maximum allowable return (the cap).

```
  $1,000,000  Previous Year's EOY Accumulated Value
+        $0  New Policy Premium
  $1,000,000  Current Year's BOY Accumulated Value
-    $50,000  Current Year's Policy Charges
    $950,000  Current Year's EOY Accumulated Value (Before Index Credit)
x      9.00%  Index Credit (assuming a +15.00% S&P 500 Return & 9.00% cap)
     $85,000  Accumulated Index Credit (Accumulated Value Gain)
+   $950,000  Current Year's EOY Accumulated Value (Before Index Credit)
  $1,035,500  Current Year's EOY Accumulated Value (After Index Credit)
```

However if the S&P 500 produced a negative return in a given year, the index credit would be 0.00% (the floor). This stop-loss feature of this particular crediting method acts as a risk-mitigation tool, which is certainly one of the most valuable elements of the *IUL* product chassis.

However, one of the most inaccurate statements I've heard some life insurance agents say is, *"With the IUL's 0.00% floor, you can never lose money."* Mathematically speaking, this is not a true statement. It is true that you would not receive a negative index return (an index return less than the 0.00% floor), however that is only true AFTER the policy charges have been deducted from the policy value. If the policy charges were $50,000 in a given year, and the *BOY* cash surrender value was $1,000,000 (assuming a 0.00% index credit in such year), the *EOY* cash surrender value would be $950,000.

	$1,000,000	Previous Year's EOY Accumulated Value
+	$0	New Policy Premium
	$1,000,000	Current Year's BOY Accumulated Value
-	$50,000	Current Year's Policy Charges
	$950,000	Current Year's EOY Accumulated Value (Before Index Credit)
x	0.00%	Index Credit (assuming a -15.00% S&P 500 Return & 0.00% floor)
	$0	Accumulated Index Credit (Accumulated Value Gain)
+	$950,000	Current Year's EOY Accumulated Value (Before Index Credit)
	$950,000	Current Year's EOY Accumulated Value (After Index Credit)

In this example, the policy's *Accumulated Value* would have actually decreased by $50,000 despite the 0.00% floor.

Aside from premium financing, the first risk factor to understand in an *IUL* is the relationship between *policy index credits* and *policy charges*.

One of the problems I have with clients making buying decisions solely based on standard carrier illustrations is that they depict a positive static index return every year with no simulations of volatility wherein 0.00% index returns are modeled (as they were in the example I just explained).

What this means is that the discussion (and mathematical modeling) of negative arbitrage during 0.00% return years is never properly articulated (and certainly never mathematically stress-tested) in most advisor/client discussions.

As I mentioned earlier in this book, one of the main things that makes me stand apart from other premium financing intermediaries is my ability to mathematically model scenarios wherein these design elements (e.g., floors, caps, charges, etc.) can be modeled during times of volatility so you can actually see the potential effects of these different variables.

I will discuss how my backtesting software models these variables (and their effects on potential outcomes) later in this book.

But first, let's discuss how the floors and caps are created by the carriers, as well as the long-term sustainability of such product features.

Chapter 5
How IUL Floors & Caps Work

The 0.00% floor sounds too good to be true, doesn't it?

Years ago when I first heard about this *IUL* feature, I thought the same thing. Most people do not truly understand how this feature actually works, and this seemingly mysterious *black box* makes intelligent people skeptical (as they should be). I am still shocked that the life insurance industry does not do a better job of explaining how the *floor & cap proposition* mechanically works in practice, because once you understand it, you will appreciate just how well thought out (and how sustainable) this design element truly is.

To understand how an *IUL*'s crediting method works, we must first discuss the origin of permanent life insurance policies in general. We will start with one type of permanent life insurance policy: *Whole Life*.

Whole Life is not synonymous with the category of ALL permanent life insurance policies. *Whole Life* is one of several different types of permanent life insurance. Compared to *Term* life insurance (which expires after the term period), *Whole Life* was originally designed to give a person life insurance coverage that would last for their whole/entire life, hence the name *Whole Life*.

The general concept was that the premiums (approximately four times greater than *Term* insurance premiums) would not only pay for the cost of insurance, but the excess premiums would be *invested* in the life insurance company itself (somewhat similar to buying stock in the insurance company – not exactly, but similar). These excess premiums invested in the life insurance company would yield a *dividend* based on how well the life insurance company's overall investment portfolio did in the previous year.

A dividend would be declared, then it would be credited to the policy's cash value the following year. The cash value would then be used to pay for the ongoing *Cost Of Insurance* (long after the insured person stopped paying premiums) which enabled the policy to last until the end of the insured person's life – insuring them for their *whole* life. To give you an idea of how stable these *Whole Life* dividends have been over time, below are the historical dividend credits over the last forty years of four major *Whole Life* carriers.

YEAR	CALENDAR YEAR	GUARDIAN DIVIDENDS	MASS MUTUAL DIVIDENDS	NORTHWESTERN DIVIDENDS	PENN MUTUAL DIVIDENDS	LOWEST DIVIDEND OF 4 CARRIERS
1	1983	7.65%	8.27%	9.75%	6.58%	6.58%
2	1984	12.25%	11.60%	10.75%	7.15%	7.15%
3	1985	13.25%	12.20%	11.00%	11.20%	11.00%
4	1986	13.25%	12.20%	11.25%	11.20%	11.20%
5	1987	12.50%	12.20%	11.00%	8.20%	8.20%
6	1988	12.00%	11.35%	10.25%	8.20%	8.20%
7	1989	11.50%	11.15%	10.00%	9.93%	9.93%
8	1990	11.00%	10.50%	10.00%	9.93%	9.93%
9	1991	10.50%	10.50%	10.00%	9.93%	9.93%
10	1992	10.25%	9.95%	9.25%	9.93%	9.25%
11	1993	9.75%	9.45%	9.25%	9.70%	9.25%
12	1994	9.00%	9.30%	8.50%	9.20%	8.50%
13	1995	8.50%	9.00%	8.50%	8.50%	8.50%
14	1996	8.00%	8.40%	8.50%	8.50%	8.00%
15	1997	8.50%	8.40%	8.50%	8.00%	8.00%
16	1998	8.75%	8.40%	8.80%	8.00%	8.00%
17	1999	8.75%	8.40%	8.80%	7.40%	7.40%
18	2000	8.50%	8.30%	8.80%	7.40%	7.40%
19	2001	8.50%	8.30%	8.80%	7.40%	7.40%
20	2002	8.00%	8.10%	8.60%	7.40%	7.40%
21	2003	7.00%	7.90%	8.20%	6.48%	6.48%
22	2004	6.60%	7.50%	7.70%	5.74%	5.74%
23	2005	6.75%	7.00%	7.50%	5.74%	5.74%
24	2006	6.50%	7.55%	7.50%	6.30%	6.30%
25	2007	6.75%	7.55%	7.50%	6.30%	6.30%
26	2008	7.25%	7.90%	7.50%	6.34%	6.34%
27	2009	7.30%	7.45%	6.50%	6.34%	6.34%
28	2010	7.00%	6.85%	6.15%	6.34%	6.15%
29	2011	6.85%	6.80%	6.00%	6.34%	6.00%
30	2012	6.95%	7.00%	5.85%	6.34%	5.85%
31	2013	6.65%	7.00%	5.60%	6.34%	5.60%
32	2014	6.25%	7.10%	5.60%	6.34%	5.60%
33	2015	6.05%	7.10%	5.60%	6.34%	5.60%
34	2016	6.05%	7.10%	5.45%	6.34%	5.45%
35	2017	5.85%	6.70%	5.00%	6.34%	5.00%
36	2018	5.85%	6.70%	5.00%	6.34%	5.00%
37	2019	5.85%	6.40%	5.00%	6.10%	5.00%
38	2020	5.65%	6.20%	6.20%	6.10%	5.65%
39	2021	5.65%	6.00%	6.00%	5.75%	5.65%
40	2022	5.65%	6.00%	5.00%	5.75%	5.00%
	AVERAGE:	8.22%	8.39%	7.88%	7.44%	7.15%

In addition, most *Whole Life* products also guarantee a minimum annual return (typically around 4.00%).

One of the main benefits of the cash value accumulation inside a life insurance policy is tax-free growth (due to IRS tax code 7702). This favorable tax treatment eventually led to the category of *permanent life insurance* expanding into several additional products with more aggressive underlying investments.

When *Variable Universal Life (VUL)* insurance products hit the market, the idea was to use mutual funds as the underlying investments instead of the life insurance carrier's guaranteed return and dividend crediting method. In concept, the client could use the same mutual funds they were already investing in, but by housing them inside a life insurance construct, the gains on these mutual funds would be tax-free.

It was a great concept in theory, especially when mutual fund returns were sky-high like they were in the mid-80's and 90's. But when the tech bubble burst in the early 2000's, it was a rude awakening for *VULs* because in order to offset the high policy expenses that were built into the *VUL* construction, the underlying mutual fund returns needed to perform as they did in the previous two decades. When this did not happen during *The Lost Decade* (2000-2009 wherein the S&P 500 produced several negative returns during this ten-year run), these expense *charges* began to outpace the *VULs' credits*. Today, many advisors and consumers have shifted their interest away from *VUL* policies towards *IUL* policies.

Unlike a *VUL* policy that can experience negative returns, *IULs* have a *floor* – a minimum index credit – which is typically 0.00%. The question is, *"How is this possible and how is this sustainable?"*

If you recall, the *Whole Life* product crediting method included a guaranteed return plus a dividend based on how profitable the life insurance company was in the previous year. In an *IUL* product, the carrier essentially takes the guaranteed return they were going to automatically credit in the *Whole Life* policy and uses that amount as the budget to purchase *options contracts*.

I am going to attempt to explain the general mechanics of how this works without getting too overly detailed, for the full explanation would require a 1,000+ page book. In my attempt to teach you the basics, I will articulate this as succinctly as possible. Additionally, in the spirit of full disclosure, there are details that vary from carrier to carrier, product to product.

For example, *Allianz* does not currently use investment banking firms to purchase their options contracts. They do it in-house due to the massive amount of options purchasing they do to support both their *IUL* products and their *Indexed Annuities*, so their method of utilizing S&P 500-correlated options contracts is different. I am not saying the *Allianz's IUL* products are necessarily better or worse than other carriers' *IULs*. I am just mentioning their unique way of buying options.

As another example of differentiation, *Pacific Life* applies their index credit to the *Average Monthly Accumulated Value*, whereas most other carriers apply their index credit to the *EOY Accumulated Value*, which is a lower value. Again, I am not saying that *Pacific Life's IUL* products are necessarily better or worse than other carriers' *IULs*. I am just mentioning their unique way calculating their index crediting method.

These are just two of many examples of how each product from each carrier is built slightly differently, however learning about *IULs* in general is best done by using one hypothetical example.

In this hypothetical example, the carrier purchases *options* from an investment banking firm – S&P 500-correlated options with a 0.00% floor. The budget for this type of arrangement is approximately 4.00% of the life insurance premium ($4,000 per $100,000 in insurance premium). But remember, that was the amount the carrier was going to automatically credit the *Whole Life* policy's cash value anyway, so in this scenario, the carrier has zero exposure because that allocation was already built into the pricing.

The investment banking firm takes the $4,000 as the *options premium*, and if the S&P 500 produces a negative return, they absorb the losses and pass the benefit of the 0.00% floor on to the carrier, who then passes the benefit on to the policy. Though the investment banking firm absorbs the loss below 0.00%, they do get to keep the $4,000 options premium.

If the S&P 500 produces a positive return, they pass that return through to the carrier, who then passes the return through to the policy, up to a maximum allowable return (the cap), and any return above the cap is then retained by the investment banking firm in addition to the $4,000 options premium per $100,000 in insurance premium.

The carrier does not incur any risk in a negative S&P 500 return scenario, and they do not participate in any of the upside above the cap either. Remember, the $4,000 options premium they paid the investment banking firm was already budgeted into the contract pricing, so for the policy owner, the decision to buy an *IUL* instead of a *Whole Life* policy is based on the belief that over time, the returns of the S&P 500-correlated index fund with a floor and cap with outpace the dividend returns of a *Whole Life* product.

This decision could be based on the client analyzing historical S&P 500 performance using the floor and cap assumptions, and comparing them to historical *Whole Life* dividend returns.

This decision could also be influenced by the conservative nature of the *Whole Life* dividend crediting history which has never produced a 0.00% return, let alone a negative return.

However, there are several elements in addition to the dividend or index return that also determine the actual cash value yield over time.

For example, policy charges need to be factored into the equation. The actual sequence of returns that a policy experiences also plays a major role in accumulation.

Another variable that affects cash value accumulation is the method in which drawdowns are taken from the policy values – not just retirement income drawdowns, but drawdowns to pay off the third-party lender in a premium financing arrangement. I will be discussing this element in great depth in the upcoming chapters.

The following chart shows historical S&P 500 returns and different floors and caps. Again, merely comparing average *Whole Life* dividends to average S&P 500-correlated *after-floor/after-cap* returns does not tell the entire story.

YEAR	CALENDAR YEAR	S&P 500 RETURNS (NO DIVIDENDS)	9.00% CAP 0.00% FLOOR	10.00% CAP 0.00% FLOOR	11.00% CAP 0.00% FLOOR	12.00% CAP 0.00% FLOOR
1	1983	17.26%	9.00%	10.00%	11.00%	12.00%
2	1984	1.38%	1.38%	1.38%	1.38%	1.38%
3	1985	26.36%	9.00%	10.00%	11.00%	12.00%
4	1986	14.62%	9.00%	10.00%	11.00%	12.00%
5	1987	2.04%	2.04%	2.04%	2.04%	2.04%
6	1988	12.39%	9.00%	10.00%	11.00%	12.00%
7	1989	27.25%	9.00%	10.00%	11.00%	12.00%
8	1990	-6.56%	0.00%	0.00%	0.00%	0.00%
9	1991	26.30%	9.00%	10.00%	11.00%	12.00%
10	1992	4.48%	4.48%	4.48%	4.48%	4.48%
11	1993	7.07%	7.07%	7.07%	7.07%	7.07%
12	1994	-1.56%	0.00%	0.00%	0.00%	0.00%
13	1995	34.13%	9.00%	10.00%	11.00%	12.00%
14	1996	20.26%	9.00%	10.00%	11.00%	12.00%
15	1997	31.01%	9.00%	10.00%	11.00%	12.00%
16	1998	26.67%	9.00%	10.00%	11.00%	12.00%
17	1999	19.53%	9.00%	10.00%	11.00%	12.00%
18	2000	-10.14%	0.00%	0.00%	0.00%	0.00%
19	2001	-13.04%	0.00%	0.00%	0.00%	0.00%
20	2002	-23.37%	0.00%	0.00%	0.00%	0.00%
21	2003	26.38%	9.00%	10.00%	11.00%	12.00%
22	2004	8.99%	8.99%	8.99%	8.99%	8.99%
23	2005	3.00%	3.00%	3.00%	3.00%	3.00%
24	2006	13.60%	9.00%	10.00%	11.00%	12.00%
25	2007	3.52%	3.52%	3.52%	3.52%	3.52%
26	2008	-38.49%	0.00%	0.00%	0.00%	0.00%
27	2009	23.65%	9.00%	10.00%	11.00%	12.00%
28	2010	12.63%	9.00%	10.00%	11.00%	12.00%
29	2011	0.10%	0.10%	0.10%	0.10%	0.10%
30	2012	13.29%	9.00%	10.00%	11.00%	12.00%
31	2013	29.43%	9.00%	10.00%	11.00%	12.00%
32	2014	11.54%	9.00%	10.00%	11.00%	11.54%
33	2015	-0.73%	0.00%	0.00%	0.00%	0.00%
34	2016	9.54%	9.00%	9.54%	9.54%	9.54%
35	2017	19.42%	9.00%	10.00%	11.00%	12.00%
36	2018	-6.24%	0.00%	0.00%	0.00%	0.00%
37	2019	28.88%	9.00%	10.00%	11.00%	12.00%
38	2020	16.26%	9.00%	10.00%	11.00%	12.00%
39	2021	26.89%	9.00%	10.00%	11.00%	12.00%
40	2022	-19.44%	0.00%	0.00%	0.00%	0.00%
Average Returns:		9.96%	5.94%	6.50%	7.05%	7.59%

What I find mildly fascinating is that when comparing the average index credits seen above (during this particular historical 40-year period) to the average *Whole Life* dividend credits shown during the same historical 40-year period (as depicted a few pages ago), the average *Whole Life* dividend credits from three of the four carriers I analyzed are better than the average *IUL's* S&P 500-correlated *after-floor/after-cap* credits, even with a 12.00% cap. However, the *after-floor/after-cap* credits in this chart do not include any bonuses that may exist in some real world *IULs*, including both *persistency bonuses* and *multiplier bonuses* (which I will discuss later in this book).

But merely comparing the average historical *Whole Life* dividend credits to the historical *IUL* index credits does not give you a complete picture of which is *better*, especially when financing the premiums.

The reason I say this is that when the third-party lender is paid off by taking a lump sum drawdown from the policy value, it can be done in three different ways in an *IUL*.

1. Withdrawals.
2. Fixed Loans.
3. Participating Loans.

Some *Whole Life* products will not allow the policy owner to drawdown policy values as efficiently as *IUL* products, and in premium financing, this is an extremely important attribute to consider for the long-term sustainability of the policy.

Yes, some *Non-Direct Recognition Whole Life* carriers allow drawdowns to be taken in a similar fashion to the way *Participating Loans* are treated in an *IUL* (currently *New York Life* and *Mass Mutual* allow this), while other *Direct Recognition Whole Life* carriers limit the drawdowns to be treated similarly to *Fixed Loans* in an *IUL*.

In the next chapter, I will explain the difference between *Withdrawals*, *Fixed Loans*, and *Participating Loans* in an *IUL*.

Chapter 6
How Policy Drawdowns Work

There are three ways to take drawdowns from an *IUL*, whether it be for supplemental retirement income or to pay off a third-party premium financing lender. You can take *Withdrawals*, *Fixed Policy Loans*, or *Participating Policy Loans*.

1. Withdrawal.

In a *withdrawal* scenario, the drawdown amount is literally withdrawn from the *Gross Accumulated Cash Value* to payoff the third-party lender. From that moment forward, the remaining *Net Accumulated Value* of the policy receives the annual *after-floor/after-cap* index credit each year.

WITHDRAWAL

① $15,000,000 WITHDRAWAL

② $25,000,000 ACCUMULATED VALUE
-$15,000,000 WITHDRAWAL
$10,000,000 ACCUMULATED VALUE

(Index Credit applied to $10,000,000)

2. Fixed Loan (AKA "Wash Loan").

When taking a *Fixed Policy Loan*, the drawdown amount is removed from the policy *Gross Accumulated Cash Value* and placed into a separate account that credits a fixed return (3.00% as a hypothetical example) instead of the annual *after-floor/after-cap* index credit each year. The carrier then "loans" the policy owner the same drawdown amount and "charges" interest on the policy loan at the same interest rate the fixed account credits (3.00% in this example), making it a *wash loan*. Similar to the *Withdrawal* scenario, from that moment forward, only the remaining *Net Accumulated Cash Value* of the policy receives the annual *after-floor/after-cap* index credit each year.

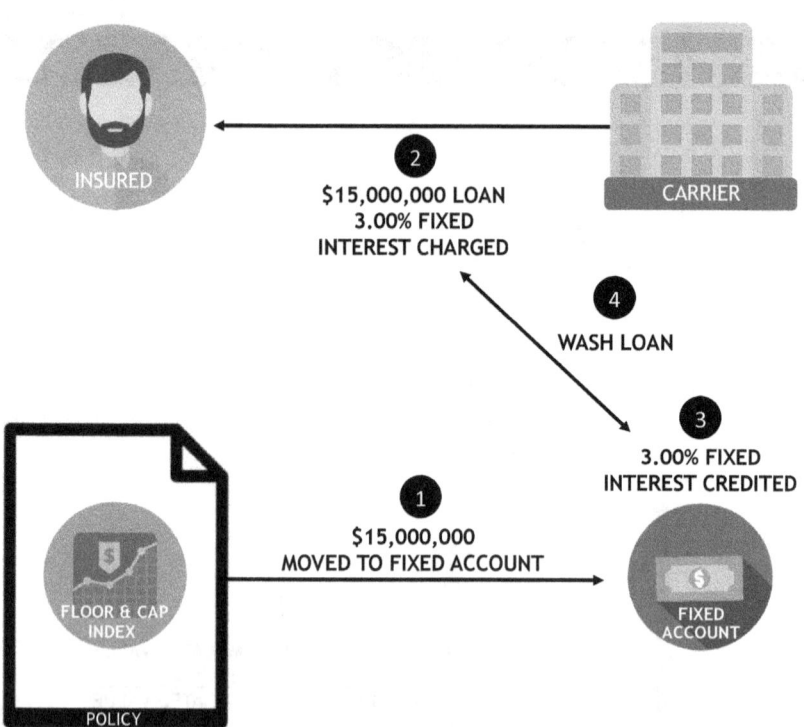

3. Participating Loan (AKA "Indexed Loan").

When taking a *Participating Policy Loan*, with some carriers, the drawdown amount is removed from the *Gross Accumulated Cash Value* and placed into a separate index account that receives the same (or similar) annual *after-floor/after-cap* index credit as the policy's *Cash Value*. With other carriers, the drawdown amount actually remains in the policy's *Gross Accumulated Cash Value*. The carrier then "loans" the policy owner the same drawdown amount and "charges" interest on this policy loan. Sometimes the interest rate charged is a fixed amount (5.00% for example), and sometimes the interest rate is a variable floating rate. In this policy loan strategy, the policy owner is hoping the *S&P 500-correlated floor & cap* index crediting method will outpace the *Participating Loan* interest charged.

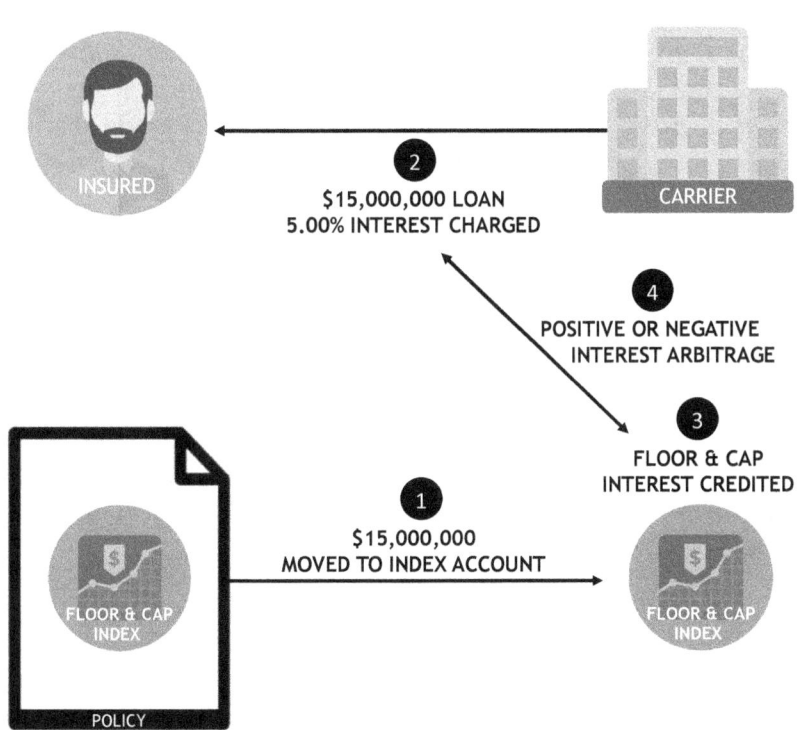

The anticipated benefit of the *Participating Loan* is that from the moment the *Participating Loan* is taken, the annual *after-floor/after-cap* index credit is applied to the *Gross Accumulated Value* in the policy, not the *Net Accumulated Value*. If the funds were moved into a separate index account (supposing the carrier of choice uses this method), these funds are also credited based on the *after-floor/after-cap* index credit methodology.

This is perhaps the most misunderstood (and undervalued) component of premium financing. The fact that the annual index credit is applied to the *Gross Accumulated Value* (not the *Net Value*) means that as the index credit is applied to the larger *gross* value.

As an example, when comparing a *Financed Policy* (after the third-party lender is paid off) to a *Non-Financed Policy*, if the *Financed Policy* had a *Gross Accumulated Value* of $7,000,000 in a given year (after charges) and a *Participating Loan* amount of $6,000,000, the *Net Cash Value* would be $1,000,000.

If the *Non-Financed Policy's Gross Accumulated Value* was the same $1,000,000 as the *Financed Policy's Net Value* in the same year, if the index credit in that year was 10%, the *Non-Financed Policy* would receive a $100,000 index credit that year (10% of the $1,000,000 cash value).

However, the *Financed Policy* would receive a $700,000 index credit that year (10% of the $7,000,000 *Gross Accumulated Value*). Of course, that would be partially offset by the *Participating Loan* interest charged, so if the *Participating Loan* rate was 5%, the $6,000,000 *Participating Loan* amount, that would result in $300,000 interest charged in that given year, making the *Net Policy Cash Value* increase by $400,000 in that year ($700,000 index credit minus $300,000 interest charged equals $400,000 net gain). That is four times the cash value gained by the *Non-Financed Policy* in that given year.

To be fair, if the S&P 500 produced a negative return in that year (which would have resulted in a 0% index credit), the *Non-Financed Policy's Cash Value* would receive zero gains after the policy charges were deducted from the cash value that year.

However with the *Financed Policy*, in addition to the charges, the $300,000 in *Participating Loan* interest would also be subtracted from the *Net Cash Value* (not the *Gross Accumulated Value*, but the *Net Cash Value*).

The accounting of this is all done on a ledger behind the scenes with the carrier, making it easy for the policy owner. In other words, the policy owner does not need to do any independent accounting to manage the interest charged and credited.

To evaluate the risk of *Participating Loans* and the potential negative arbitrage between the loan interest charged and the 0% index credited in given years, my backtesting software analyzes 121 different historical 40-year periods of S&P 500 performance, builds a *proxy* for the premium financed *IUL* with the *Participating Loan* component, and models the 40-year period that produced the *Worst Compounded Annual Growth Rate* of the 121 different historical 40-year periods, for this is the type of scenario wherein the *Participating Loan* proposition might incur a negative outcome.

During the challenging 40-year sequence, we evaluate the relationship between the *Participating Loan* interest accrued versus the gains made by keeping the payoff amount in the policy's *Gross Accumulated Value* (or separate index account if the carrier uses such methodology). Over such time, if the debt outpaces the growth on such *Participating Loan* funds, it would be prudent for the client to make their decisions based on whether or not they want to incur that risk, despite how much more profitable such proposition may be during better index performing times. I always provide this analytical report to my clients and review it with them.

If the 40-year period that produced the *Worst Compounded Annual Growth Rate* of the 121 different historical 40-year periods shows a net gain in such *Participating Loan* proposition, that stress-test becomes just as valuable in the client's overall education and awareness.

To be clear, this evaluation model is not a modified version of an *IUL* illustration. That would violate AG-49A guidelines and several other compliance regulations. I created a *Hypothetical Synthetic Asset* – a fictitious index account – that behaves very similar to an *IUL* in regards to charges, crediting methodology, and participating loan methodology.

The goal is to see how these factors could potentially affect short-term and long-term outcomes during times of volatility. For example, in certain sequences of returns we analyze, there are several consecutive 0.00% index credits within the first ten years of the 40-year sequence.

In other scenarios we model, the consecutive 0.00% index returns happen in the middle of the 40-year sequence during the beginning years of income drawdowns (or right before or after the lender payoff, similar to a premium financed life insurance scenario), both of which put excessive stress on cash value accumulation which is needed to keep the policy in force.

In an effort to be extremely clear in this discussion, the scenario that I called *"the 40-year period that produced the Worst Compounded Annual Growth Rate of the 121 different historical 40-year periods analyzed"* is not the worst possible 40-year outcome imaginable. It is just the worst one of the 121 different periods I analyzed. It is within the realm of possibility that the next forty years could be even worse than the *Worst 40-Year Period* out of these 121 periods I analyzed, just as it is possible that the next forty years could produce an even better outcome than the *Best 40-Year Period* I analyzed.

Perhaps this overly granular explanation is painfully redundant, however I believe it is important to communicate in a crystal clear manner so it is virtually impossible to misinterpret my mathematical findings.

Before we delve into my backtesting methodology, in this next chapter, I will address one of the most controversial topics of discussion when it comes to *IULs*: *Multiplier Bonuses & Asset-Based Charges*.

Chapter 7
Are IUL Multiplier Bonuses Too Risky?

One of the most controversial design elements in modern-day *IULs* is the *Multiplier Bonus*. At the moment, the majority of *IUL* multiplier propositions allow a client to accept an additional asset-based charge in exchange for a multiplier bonus that enhances the index return.

In this arrangement, the client *doubles down* on the carrier's ability to buy more options contracts from the investment bankers. Often times, *IUL* critics accuse *IUL Multipliers* of being opaque, mysterious, and expensive, however the multiplier proposition is actually quite simple.

As an example, if the multiplier bonus factor is 1.45X, this means that the *after-floor/after-cap* index return would be multiplied by 1.45, giving the pre-multiplier return a 45.00% boost.

```
        15.00%  End-Of-Segment S&P 500 Return
   ≥    10.00%  IUL Cap
        10.00%  End-Of-Segment After-Floor/After-Cap Return
   x     1.45   Multiplier Bonus
        14.50%  EOY Index Credit After Multiplier Bonus
```

If the client likes this proposition, they can elect to purchase this feature each year at policy renewal for an asset-based charge. For example, if the asset-based multiplier charge is 1.00%, that means the policy receives an additional charge on top of the standard policy charges, calculated by multiplying 1.00% by the *Accumulated Value* and deducted from the *Accumulated Value* in the current year (1/12 of 1.00%, monthly).

Pre-AG-49A, one of the biggest criticisms of these multiplier features was that the carrier illustration depicted a static positive index credit each year, which illustrated a multiplier advantage each year. In other words, if the carrier illustration showed a static 5.50% index return every year, and the multiplier bonus factor was 1.45X, the illustration's cash value growth in the

45

illustration was actually calculated based on a 7.98% index credit (5.50% x 1.45 = 7.98%), not the stated 5.50%.

Using the static positive index credits in a carrier's illustration was misleading because in a real-world scenario, the S&P 500 is going to experience some negative return years wherein the policy's index credit would be 0.00%. In these years, not only would the policy's cash value decrease due to the standard policy charges, but the additional 1.00% multiplier asset-based charge would create an additional reduction in cash value.

The *IUL* multiplier critics and die-hard *Whole Life* fans accused *IUL* illustrations of being misleading because the illustrations assumed a positive multiplier bonus each year, not taking into consideration the substantial reduction in cash value the additional asset-based charges could cause during 0.00% index crediting years, and they were right… sort of.

The problem was that no one did the math.

The critics were making broad conceptual assertations that the multiplier propositions were too risky and the asset-based charges too costly, but they had no mathematically-proven analytics to back up their claims.

On the other side of the fence were the over-zealous *IUL* fanatics that reveled in showing the massively bolstered returns and claimed that *IUL*s with multiplier bonuses were the best thing since sliced bread, but they had no mathematically-proven analytics to back up their claims either.

So who was right?

Neither of them.

As a result, the regulators passed a new actuarial guideline – AG-49A – that restricted carrier illustrations from illustrating multiplier bonuses. The illustrations could now only show multiplier asset-based charges, but no multiplier bonuses. The nonsensical nature of this restriction didn't solve the problem they were trying to solve.

I would agree that an illustration that depicts a positive static return every year wherein a multiplier bonus enhances the index return *every year* tells a very incomplete and inaccurate story of how multiplier *IULs* actually work, but I would also say that showing a carrier illustration with multiplier asset-based charges with no multiplier bonus credits also tells a very inaccurate story.

As a result of the illogical way this restriction was implemented, most agents started running illustrations *without* any multiplier features. The problem with this decision was that if the client intended to buy an *IUL* with a multiplier feature, the agent was showing the client something they were not actually going to buy. This is perhaps the most inaccurate scenario of all scenarios an agent could present to a client.

To complicate things even further, if the client was actually going to buy an *IUL* with a multiplier feature, and they were originally shown an illustration without the multiplier feature, just prior to policy delivery, the client had to sign a version of the illustration that included all the product features they were actually buying, which included the multiplier feature. This meant that the agent had to re-run the illustration and include the multiplier asset-based charges, which then depicted a much worse cash value accumulation outcome because the additional charges eroded the as-illustrated *Cash Value* with no multiplier bonus enhancement taken into consideration. This version of the illustration looked substantially worse than the first version the client saw when they initially made their decision to buy, which made the agent look like they had *bait-and-switched* the offering.

As an alternative, the agent could have just started off showing the client a version of the illustration that included all of the multiplier charges (but did not include any of the multiplier benefits), and say, *"Trust me, there are multiplier bonuses included, but I can't show them in the carrier illustration."*

That would be like trying to sell a *$550,000 Lamborghini Aventador* that actually puts out 770 horsepower, despite the brochure stating that it only puts out 570 horsepower, and telling the client, *"Trust me, not the brochure."*

The third option the agent had was to not sell any *IULs* with multiplier bonus features whatsoever, restricting the client from buying something that might be tremendously beneficial to their overall estate plan, retirement plan, and overall financial plan. Clearly, this was not a good option either.

I am a big supporter of compliance and industry regulation in general, for I believe the spirit of *regulated compliance* is rooted in consumer protection, and consumer protection is a good thing.

But AG-49A did not solve the problem of *lack of transparency* in carrier illustrations. It just exchanged one problem for another – exchanging one inaccurate depiction for another inaccurate depiction. The illustrative limitations and inaccuracies that AG-49A created didn't stop there either.

AG-49A also required the carrier illustration to depict a static *Participating Loan Rate* equal to 0.50% less than the index crediting rate illustrated, despite what the actual *Participating Loan Rate* was. In other words, if the carrier illustration assumed a 5.75% index crediting rate, the *Participating Loan Rate* had to be illustrated at 5.25%, even if the actual *Participating Loan Rate* was only 5.00%.

This problem was two-fold.

First, this depiction showed a *Participating Loan Rate* that was not accurate. And second, because the illustration depicted a positive static index credit every year, there was always a positive arbitrage between the index credit and the *Participating Loan Rate*, which will not happen in years when the actual *Index Credit* is lower than the actual *Participating Loan Rate*.

In a year wherein the *Participating Loan Rate* was 5.00% and the index credit was 2.00%, the client would actually lose 3.00% in that negative arbitrage year (2.00% - 5.00% = -3.00%). However if the *Participating Loan Rate* was 5.00%, and the index credit was 9.00%, the client would actually gain 4.00% in that positive arbitrage year (9.00% - 5.00% = 4.00%).

This is why my backtesting software's capabilities are so valuable, because they can mathematically articulate both types of scenarios in each given year so the client can actually see how the math works during times of volatility. I will explain these capabilities in the next chapter.

Chapter 8
Why Backtesting Is So Important

So far, I have discussed the problems I see with the assumptions and limitations depicted in carrier illustrations, as well as how *IUL* crediting and charges methods actually work in real-world scenarios. In this chapter, I will explore how floors, caps, multipliers and asset-based charges can impact financial outcomes. I will do so by reviewing a case study using data sourced directly from an actual premium financed *IUL* policy, but I will do so by analyzing the behavior of a *Leveraged Hypothetical Synthetic Asset* that will act as a proxy for a *Premium Financed IUL* (hereinafter called *The Proxy*.

When I started developing my proprietary backtesting software over a decade ago, I had no idea it would evolve into what it is today. Its capabilities of deconstructing an IUL's chassis, measuring risk during times of volatility, and testing the efficacy of different product designs is truly unparalleled.

As I stated earlier in this book, my process begins with analyzing 121 different historical 40-year periods. I use one-year annual point-to-point segments and track them over 40-year rolling periods.

The first 40-year period I analyzed started on January 1, 1970 and tracked historical S&P 500 performance for the next forty years (forty 12-month segments), ending on December 31, 2009. The second 40-year period I analyzed started one month later on February 1, 1970 and ended on January 31, 2010. The third one started one month after that on March 1, 1970 and ended on February 28, 2010. These 40-year sequences continued with the 121st one starting on January 1, 1980 and ending on December 31, 2019.

In the spirit of conservatism (and arguably pessimism), I will focus on the 40-year period that produced the *Worst Compounded Annual Growth Rate* of all the 121 different 40-year periods analyzed. To be clear, this particular 40-year period was only the "worst" one based on the *Compounded Annual Growth Rates* of the 121 different 40-year periods I analyzed, not the *"worst possible case scenario that could ever exist in the future."*

It is certainly possible that the next forty years could produce an even worse *Compounded Annual Growth Rate* than this sequence, and it is also possible that the next forty years could

4 BACKTESTED YEAR	5 INDEX GROSS RETURN	6 INDEX CREDIT		7 MULTIPLIER BONUS (x)		8 INDEX CREDIT w/MULTIPLIER		9 PERSISTENCY BONUS (+)		10 TOTAL INDEX CREDIT (%)
1971	12.42%	9.00%	x	1.00	=	9.00%	+	0.00%	=	9.00%
1972	-1.92%	0.00%	x	1.45	=	0.00%	+	0.00%	=	0.00%
1973	-41.40%	0.00%	x	1.45	=	0.00%	+	0.00%	=	0.00%
1974	32.00%	9.00%	x	1.45	=	11.15%	+	0.00%	=	11.15%
1975	25.48%	9.00%	x	1.45	=	11.15%	+	0.00%	=	11.15%
1976	-8.28%	0.00%	x	1.45	=	0.00%	+	0.00%	=	0.00%
1977	6.23%	6.23%	x	1.45	=	9.03%	+	0.00%	=	9.03%
1978	6.61%	6.61%	x	1.45	=	9.59%	+	0.00%	=	9.59%
1979	14.76%	9.00%	x	1.45	=	11.15%	+	0.00%	=	11.15%
1980	-7.40%	0.00%	x	1.45	=	0.00%	+	0.00%	=	0.00%
1981	3.65%	3.65%	x	1.45	=	5.29%	+	0.00%	=	5.29%
1982	37.91%	9.00%	x	1.45	=	11.15%	+	0.00%	=	11.15%
1983	0.02%	0.02%	x	1.45	=	0.03%	+	0.00%	=	0.03%
1984	9.62%	9.00%	x	1.45	=	11.15%	+	0.00%	=	11.15%
1985	27.04%	9.00%	x	1.45	=	11.15%	+	0.00%	=	11.15%
1986	39.13%	9.00%	x	1.45	=	11.15%	+	0.00%	=	11.15%
1987	-15.51%	0.00%	x	1.45	=	0.00%	+	0.00%	=	0.00%
1988	28.41%	9.00%	x	1.45	=	11.15%	+	0.00%	=	11.15%
1989	-12.34%	0.00%	x	1.45	=	0.00%	+	0.00%	=	0.00%
1990	26.73%	9.00%	x	1.45	=	11.15%	+	0.00%	=	11.15%
1991	7.72%	7.72%	x	1.45	=	11.15%	+	0.00%	=	11.15%
1992	9.84%	9.00%	x	1.45	=	11.15%	+	0.00%	=	11.15%
1993	0.82%	0.82%	x	1.45	=	1.19%	+	0.00%	=	1.19%
1994	26.30%	9.00%	x	1.45	=	11.15%	+	0.00%	=	11.15%
1995	17.61%	9.00%	x	1.45	=	11.15%	+	0.00%	=	11.15%
1996	37.82%	9.00%	x	1.45	=	11.15%	+	0.00%	=	11.15%
1997	7.36%	7.36%	x	1.45	=	10.67%	+	0.00%	=	10.67%
1998	26.13%	9.00%	x	1.45	=	11.15%	+	0.00%	=	11.15%
1999	11.99%	9.00%	x	1.45	=	11.15%	+	0.00%	=	11.15%
2000	-27.54%	0.00%	x	1.45	=	0.00%	+	0.00%	=	0.00%
2001	-21.68%	0.00%	x	1.45	=	0.00%	+	0.00%	=	0.00%
2002	22.16%	9.00%	x	1.45	=	11.15%	+	0.00%	=	11.15%
2003	11.91%	9.00%	x	1.45	=	11.15%	+	0.00%	=	11.15%
2004	10.25%	9.00%	x	1.45	=	11.15%	+	0.00%	=	11.15%
2005	8.71%	8.71%	x	1.45	=	11.15%	+	0.00%	=	11.15%
2006	14.29%	9.00%	x	1.45	=	11.15%	+	0.00%	=	11.15%
2007	-23.61%	0.00%	x	1.45	=	0.00%	+	0.00%	=	0.00%
2008	-9.37%	0.00%	x	1.45	=	0.00%	+	0.00%	=	0.00%
2009	7.96%	7.96%	x	1.45	=	11.15%	+	0.00%	=	11.15%
2010	-0.86%	0.00%	x	1.45	=	0.00%	+	0.00%	=	0.00%

produce an even better *Compounded Annual Growth Rate* than the *Best 40-Year Period* of the 121 different 40-year periods I analyzed.

This particular 40-year historical period analyzed in this chart started on October 1, 1971 (column 4) and produced the *Worst Compounded Annual Growth Rate* of all the 121 different 40-year periods analyzed. These historical S&P 500 returns do not include S&P 500 dividends (column 5), and I am modeling a 9.00% hypothetical pre-multiplier cap (column 6). I am also modeling a 1.45X multiplier bonus (column 7) with a 1.00% asset-based multiplier charge (I will explain how this asset-based charge works later in this chapter). The 1.45X multiplier bonus was then accounted for in the *Index Credit w/ Multiplier* (column 8) which is the *after-floor/after-cap/after-multiplier* return.

In a year wherein the index return hits the 9.00% cap, the *Index Credit w/ Multiplier* is 11.15% because this crediting methodology has a maximum allowable return of 2.15% above the cap (9.00% + 2.15% = 11.15%) despite 9.00% x 1.45 = 13.05%.

Some policies have a *Persistency Bonus* (column 9) which is then added to the *Index Credit w/ Multiplier* return, which equals the *Total Index Credit* (column 10). In this particular product modeled on the previous page, there is no *Persistency Bonus*.

It is important to note that in the first ten years of this 40-year sequence, the S&P 500 produced several negative returns, resulting in several 0.00% *Effective Index Returns* (an extremely poor sequence of returns).

Because the *The Proxy* depicted here is not a life insurance illustration (it is just a proxy for a *Premium Financed IUL*), there is no death benefit shown, for this is not a life insurance policy. However, because we are using the same fee structure as the charges in an actual *IUL* policy, as well as the same crediting structure as an actual IUL, the behavior of this *The Proxy* gives us some perspective regarding how a *Premium Financed IUL's Cash Value* might behave during the various 40-year sequences analyzed. This is a valuable depiction to consider because the charges and crediting methods used cause the ongoing net performance to behave very similar to an actual *Premium Financed IUL*.

The reason this *Proxy* modeling is so important – even in a death benefit-focused case – is that a real world *Premium Financed IUL's* long-term sustainability is largely based on its *Cash Value's* ability to pay the future insurance charges AND outpace the compounding *Participating Loan* debt balance with the carrier.

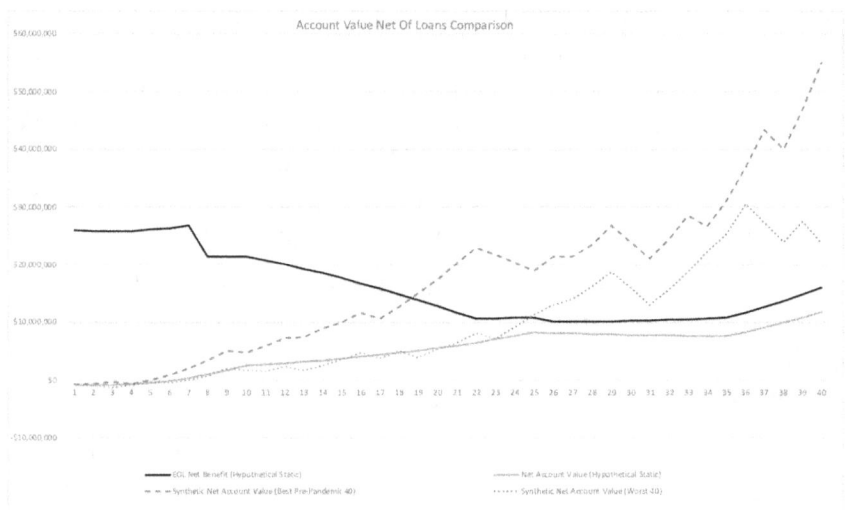

I include this graph (above) in all of my client proposals because it compares the net *Cash Surrender Value* as-illustrated in the carrier illustration (the solid grey line) to the simulated net account values in *The Proxy* during the 40-year period with the *Best Compounded Annual Growth Rate* (the heavily dashed line) and during the 40-year period with the *Worst Compounded Annual Growth Rate* (the dotted line).

Though this graph is merely a hypothetical simulation, it is interesting that even during the *Worst 40-Year Period* of the 121 different 40-year periods analyzed, the simulated account value of *The Proxy* (the dotted line) is similar to the as-illustrated *Cash Surrender Value* in the carrier illustration (the solid grey line) for the first twenty-four years.

If the values depicted in the dotted line are equal-or-greater than the *Cash Surrender Value* as depicted in the carrier illustration, it would be logical to assume that the *Death Benefit* would be equal-

or-greater than the as-illustrated *Death Benefit* in the carrier illustration for the first twenty-three years.

Furthermore, beyond the twenty-fourth year, the account value of *The Proxy* not only pulls ahead of the as-illustrated *Cash Surrender Value*, but it also eclipses the carrier as-illustrated *Net Death Benefit* (the solid black line) in both the *Best 40* and the *Worst 40*, and if the *Net Cash Surrender Value* in a real world *IUL* equaled values depicted in the dotted line, the actual *Net Death Benefit* (the solid black line) would have to be greater than the dotted line because the *Net Death Benefit* in a real world *IUL* cannot be less than the policy's *Net Cash Surrender Value*.

This particular synthetic case study is quite encouraging because the backtesting graph on the previous page depicts the outcomes represented in the carrier illustration as being substantially worse than *The Proxy* during the 40-year period with the *Worst Compounded Annual Growth Rate* out of the 121 different 40-year periods analyzed.

In addition, *The Proxy* also transparently shows both the standard charges (using the same charge amounts in the carrier illustration) as well as the additional asset-based multiplier charges and compares the total charges to the total index credits each year (depicted in the next two pages).

# YEAR	1 ASSET-BASED CHARGES (%)	2 ASSET-BASED CHARGES ($)	3 FIXED CHARGES ($)	4 BACKTESTED YEAR	5 INDEX GROSS RETURN	6 INDEX CREDIT	7 MULTIPLIER BONUS (x)			8 INDEX CREDIT w/ MULTIPLIER	+	9 PERSISTENCY BONUS (+)
1	1.00%	-$1,978	-$70,872	1971	12.42%	9.00%	x	1.00	=	9.00%	+	0.00%
2	1.00%	-$3,292	-$76,017	1972	-1.92%	0.00%	x	1.45	=	0.00%	+	0.00%
3	1.00%	-$10,663	-$123,929	1973	-41.40%	0.00%	x	1.45	=	0.00%	+	0.00%
4	1.00%	-$18,076	-$132,183	1974	32.00%	9.00%	x	1.45	=	11.15%	+	0.00%
5	1.00%	-$27,312	-$140,548	1975	25.48%	9.00%	x	1.45	=	11.15%	+	0.00%
6	1.00%	-$37,362	-$154,009	1976	-8.28%	0.00%	x	1.45	=	0.00%	+	0.00%
7	1.00%	-$44,196	-$164,296	1977	6.23%	6.23%	x	1.45	=	9.03%	+	0.00%
8	1.00%	-$54,778	-$175,745	1978	6.61%	6.61%	x	1.45	=	9.59%	+	0.00%
9	1.00%	-$66,375	-$188,310	1979	14.76%	9.00%	x	1.45	=	11.15%	+	0.00%
10	1.00%	-$79,841	-$202,052	1980	-7.40%	0.00%	x	1.45	=	0.00%	+	0.00%
11	1.00%	-$78,034	-$105,278	1981	3.65%	3.65%	x	1.45	=	5.29%	+	0.00%
12	1.00%	-$80,241	-$109,131	1982	37.91%	9.00%	x	1.45	=	11.15%	+	0.00%
13	1.00%	-$87,127	-$112,586	1983	0.02%	0.02%	x	1.45	=	0.03%	+	0.00%
14	1.00%	-$85,138	-$115,479	1984	9.62%	9.00%	x	1.45	=	11.15%	+	0.00%
15	1.00%	-$92,454	-$117,749	1985	27.04%	9.00%	x	1.45	=	11.15%	+	0.00%
16	1.00%	-$100,734	-$69,344	1986	39.13%	9.00%	x	1.45	=	11.15%	+	0.00%
17	1.00%	-$110,115	-$69,155	1987	-15.51%	0.00%	x	1.45	=	0.00%	+	0.00%
18	1.00%	-$108,330	-$67,499	1988	28.41%	9.00%	x	1.45	=	11.15%	+	0.00%
19	1.00%	-$118,511	-$63,737	1989	-12.34%	0.00%	x	1.45	=	0.00%	+	0.00%
20	1.00%	-$116,722	-$57,019	1990	26.73%	9.00%	x	1.45	=	11.15%	+	0.00%
21	1.00%	-$127,894	-$45,721	1991	7.72%	7.72%	x	1.45	=	11.15%	+	0.00%
22	1.00%	-$140,331	-$29,446	1992	9.84%	9.00%	x	1.45	=	11.15%	+	0.00%
23	1.00%	-$154,149	-$21,250	1993	0.82%	0.82%	x	1.45	=	1.19%	+	0.00%
24	1.00%	-$154,195	-$25,440	1994	26.30%	9.00%	x	1.45	=	11.15%	+	0.00%
25	1.00%	-$169,382	-$29,999	1995	17.61%	9.00%	x	1.45	=	11.15%	+	0.00%
26	1.00%	-$186,040	-$35,789	1996	37.82%	9.00%	x	1.45	=	11.15%	+	0.00%
27	1.00%	-$204,309	-$41,539	1997	7.36%	7.36%	x	1.45	=	10.67%	+	0.00%
28	1.00%	-$223,385	-$48,113	1998	26.13%	9.00%	x	1.45	=	11.15%	+	0.00%
29	1.00%	-$245,264	-$55,606	1999	11.99%	9.00%	x	1.45	=	11.15%	+	0.00%
30	1.00%	-$269,255	-$64,127	2000	-27.54%	0.00%	x	1.45	=	0.00%	+	0.00%
31	1.00%	-$265,869	-$74,583	2001	-21.68%	0.00%	x	1.45	=	0.00%	+	0.00%
32	1.00%	-$262,409	-$85,641	2002	22.16%	9.00%	x	1.45	=	11.15%	+	0.00%
33	1.00%	-$287,784	-$98,267	2003	11.91%	9.00%	x	1.45	=	11.15%	+	0.00%
34	1.00%	-$315,562	-$112,917	2004	10.25%	9.00%	x	1.45	=	11.15%	+	0.00%
35	1.00%	-$345,964	-$129,715	2005	8.71%	8.71%	x	1.45	=	11.15%	+	0.00%
36	1.00%	-$379,232	-$148,137	2006	14.29%	9.00%	x	1.45	=	11.15%	+	0.00%
37	1.00%	-$415,801	-$135,420	2007	-23.61%	0.00%	x	1.45	=	0.00%	+	0.00%
38	1.00%	-$410,390	-$115,066	2008	-9.37%	0.00%	x	1.45	=	0.00%	+	0.00%
39	1.00%	-$405,281	-$85,970	2009	7.96%	7.96%	x	1.45	=	11.15%	+	0.00%
40	1.00%	-$445,254	-$46,721	2010	-0.86%	0.00%	x	1.45	=	0.00%	+	0.00%

As you see, column 11 shows what the index credits would have been in each year in dollar amounts. In years wherein the index credited 0.00%, the cash value would obviously receive a $0 credit. Column 12 shows what the total charges would have been based on the as-illustrated charges shown in the carrier illustration, plus what any additional asset-based charges would have been based on the accumulated value during this particular backtested period. Then, column 13 shows what the net gain-or-loss would have been – the combination of any index credits received, offset by the total charges in that given year. In the years wherein the S&P 500 produced a negative return and the *Effective Index Credit* was 0.00%, this *Charges+Credits+Bonuses Report* also shows the reduction in account value during these years (column 13).

PREMIUM FINANCED LIFE INSURANCE

10 TOTAL INDEX CREDIT (%)	11 TOTAL INDEX CREDITS $	12 TOTAL CHARGES $	13 YEAR-END GAIN/LOSS $	14 EOY VALUE AFTER CHARGES B4 CREDIT	15 EOY GROSS INDEX ACCUMULATED VALUE	16 EOY INDEX VALUE NET OF NT & EXT LOANS
9.00%	$13,244	($72,850)	($59,606)	$147,150	$160,394	-$23
0.00%	$0	($79,309)	($79,309)	$301,085	$301,085	$117,425
0.00%	$0	($134,592)	($134,592)	$1,046,493	$1,046,493	$218,653
11.15%	$198,050	($150,259)	$47,791	$1,776,234	$1,974,284	$468,848
11.15%	$299,536	($167,860)	$131,676	$2,686,424	$2,985,960	$764,127
0.00%	$0	($191,371)	($191,371)	$3,674,589	$3,674,589	$695,373
9.03%	$392,355	($208,492)	$183,863	$4,346,097	$4,738,453	$952,868
9.59%	$516,567	($230,523)	$286,044	$5,387,930	$5,904,496	$1,257,493
11.15%	$728,074	($254,685)	$473,388	$6,529,811	$7,257,885	$1,687,672
0.00%	$0	($281,893)	($281,893)	$7,855,992	$7,855,992	**$1,293,340**
5.29%	$406,022	($183,312)	$222,710	$7,672,681	$8,078,702	$771,382
11.15%	$879,660	($189,372)	$690,288	$7,889,330	$8,768,990	$1,110,918
0.03%	$2,245	($199,713)	($197,468)	$8,569,277	$8,571,522	$545,863
11.15%	$933,356	($200,617)	$732,739	$8,370,905	$9,304,261	$893,370
11.15%	$1,013,987	($210,203)	$803,785	$9,094,058	$10,108,046	$1,293,432
11.15%	$1,108,083	($170,078)	$938,006	$9,937,968	$11,046,051	$1,808,336
0.00%	$0	($179,270)	($179,270)	$10,866,782	$10,866,782	$1,185,656
11.15%	$1,192,041	($175,829)	$1,016,212	$10,690,952	$11,882,994	$1,737,174
0.00%	$0	($182,248)	($182,248)	$11,700,745	$11,700,745	$1,067,926
11.15%	$1,285,261	($173,741)	$1,111,520	$11,527,004	$12,812,265	**$1,669,071**
11.15%	$1,409,209	($173,615)	$1,235,594	$12,638,650	$14,047,859	$2,369,792
11.15%	$1,547,406	($169,777)	$1,377,629	$13,878,082	$15,425,488	$3,186,873
1.19%	$182,132	($175,399)	$6,733	$15,250,089	$15,432,221	$2,375,593
11.15%	$1,700,663	($179,635)	$1,521,028	$15,252,586	$16,953,249	$3,039,343
11.15%	$1,868,056	($199,381)	$1,668,675	$16,753,868	$18,621,924	$3,809,590
11.15%	$2,051,611	($221,829)	$1,829,781	$18,400,095	$20,451,706	$4,697,819
10.67%	$2,156,684	($245,848)	$1,910,835	$20,205,857	$22,362,541	$5,621,908
11.15%	$2,463,151	($271,498)	$2,191,653	$22,091,043	$24,554,194	$6,779,451
11.15%	$2,704,246	($300,870)	$2,403,376	$24,253,324	$26,957,570	$8,099,079
0.00%	$0	($333,382)	($333,382)	$26,624,188	$26,624,188	**$6,629,930**
0.00%	$0	($340,452)	($340,452)	$26,283,736	$26,283,736	$5,099,193
11.15%	$2,891,829	($348,050)	$2,543,779	$25,935,686	$28,827,515	$6,395,554
11.15%	$3,171,223	($386,051)	$2,785,172	$28,441,464	$31,612,687	$8,103,992
11.15%	$3,477,039	($428,479)	$3,048,560	$31,184,208	$34,661,247	$10,024,135
11.15%	$3,811,691	($475,679)	$3,336,012	$34,185,568	$37,997,259	$12,177,566
11.15%	$4,177,893	($527,369)	$3,650,524	$37,469,890	$41,647,783	$14,588,744
0.00%	$0	($551,221)	($551,221)	$41,096,562	$41,096,562	$12,738,689
0.00%	$0	($525,456)	($525,456)	$40,571,106	$40,571,106	$10,852,055
11.15%	$4,468,904	($491,251)	$3,977,653	$40,079,855	$44,548,759	$13,403,193
0.00%	$0	($491,975)	($491,975)	$44,056,784	$44,056,784	**$11,416,231**

The Proxy's Charges+Credits+Bonuses Report uncovers a vitally important truth about the multiplier proposition in this particular case study, especially during this extremely adverse 40-year period. The *Asset-Based Charge* is 1.00% (column 1) for the 1.45X *Multiplier Bonus* (column 7). In *The Proxy*, the previous year's *EOY Gross Index Account Value* (column 15 of the previous year) minus 50% of the *Fixed Charges* is calculated (since the charges are monthly charges), then the 1.00% asset-based multiplier charge is applied to this value, equaling the *Asset-Based Charges ($)* in that given year (column 2).

55

# YEAR	1 ASSET-BASED CHARGES (%)	2 ASSET-BASED CHARGES ($)	3 FIXED CHARGES ($)	4 BACKTESTED YEAR	5 INDEX GROSS RETURN	6 INDEX CREDIT		7 MULTIPLIER BONUS (x)		8 INDEX CREDIT w/ MULTIPLIER		9 PERSISTENCY BONUS (+)
1	1.00%	-$1,978	-$70,872	1971	12.42%	9.00%	x	1.00	=	9.00%	+	0.00%
2	1.00%	-$3,292	-$76,017	1972	-1.92%	0.00%	x	1.45	=	0.00%	+	0.00%
3	1.00%	-$10,663	-$123,929	1973	-41.40%	0.00%	x	1.45	=	0.00%	+	0.00%
4	1.00%	-$18,076	-$132,183	1974	32.00%	9.00%	x	1.45	=	11.15%	+	0.00%
5	1.00%	-$27,312	-$140,548	1975	25.48%	9.00%	x	1.45	=	11.15%	+	0.00%
6	1.00%	-$37,362	-$154,009	1976	-8.28%	0.00%	x	1.45	=	0.00%	+	0.00%
7	1.00%	-$44,196	-$164,296	1977	6.23%	6.23%	x	1.45	=	9.03%	+	0.00%
8	1.00%	-$54,778	-$175,745	1978	6.61%	6.61%	x	1.45	=	9.59%	+	0.00%
9	1.00%	-$66,375	-$188,310	1979	14.76%	9.00%	x	1.45	=	11.15%	+	0.00%
10	1.00%	-$79,841	-$202,052	1980	-7.40%	0.00%	x	1.45	=	0.00%	+	0.00%
11	1.00%	-$78,034	-$105,278	1981	3.65%	3.65%	x	1.45	=	5.29%	+	0.00%
12	1.00%	-$80,241	-$109,131	1982	37.91%	9.00%	x	1.45	=	11.15%	+	0.00%
13	1.00%	-$87,127	-$112,586	1983	0.02%	0.02%	x	1.45	=	0.03%	+	0.00%
14	1.00%	-$85,138	-$115,479	1984	9.62%	9.00%	x	1.45	=	11.15%	+	0.00%
15	1.00%	-$92,454	-$117,749	1985	27.04%	9.00%	x	1.45	=	11.15%	+	0.00%
16	1.00%	-$100,734	-$69,344	1986	39.13%	9.00%	x	1.45	=	11.15%	+	0.00%
17	1.00%	-$110,115	-$69,155	1987	-15.51%	0.00%	x	1.45	=	0.00%	+	0.00%
18	1.00%	-$108,330	-$67,499	1988	28.41%	9.00%	x	1.45	=	11.15%	+	0.00%
19	1.00%	-$118,511	-$63,737	1989	-12.34%	0.00%	x	1.45	=	0.00%	+	0.00%
20	1.00%	-$116,722	-$57,019	1990	26.73%	9.00%	x	1.45	=	11.15%	+	0.00%
21	1.00%	-$127,894	-$45,721	1991	7.72%	7.72%	x	1.45	=	11.15%	+	0.00%
22	1.00%	-$140,331	-$29,446	1992	9.84%	9.00%	x	1.45	=	11.15%	+	0.00%
23	1.00%	-$154,149	-$21,250	1993	0.82%	0.82%	x	1.45	=	1.19%	+	0.00%
24	1.00%	-$154,195	-$25,440	1994	26.30%	9.00%	x	1.45	=	11.15%	+	0.00%
25	1.00%	-$169,382	-$29,999	1995	17.61%	9.00%	x	1.45	=	11.15%	+	0.00%
26	1.00%	-$186,040	-$35,789	1996	37.82%	9.00%	x	1.45	=	11.15%	+	0.00%
27	1.00%	-$204,309	-$41,539	1997	7.36%	7.36%	x	1.45	=	10.67%	+	0.00%
28	1.00%	-$223,385	-$48,113	1998	26.13%	9.00%	x	1.45	=	11.15%	+	0.00%
29	1.00%	-$245,264	-$55,606	1999	11.99%	9.00%	x	1.45	=	11.15%	+	0.00%
30	1.00%	-$269,255	-$64,127	2000	-27.54%	0.00%	x	1.45	=	0.00%	+	0.00%
31	1.00%	-$265,869	-$74,583	2001	-21.68%	0.00%	x	1.45	=	0.00%	+	0.00%
32	1.00%	-$262,409	-$85,641	2002	22.16%	9.00%	x	1.45	=	11.15%	+	0.00%
33	1.00%	-$287,784	-$98,267	2003	11.91%	9.00%	x	1.45	=	11.15%	+	0.00%
34	1.00%	-$315,562	-$112,917	2004	10.25%	9.00%	x	1.45	=	11.15%	+	0.00%
35	1.00%	-$345,964	-$129,715	2005	8.71%	8.71%	x	1.45	=	11.15%	+	0.00%
36	1.00%	-$379,232	-$148,137	2006	14.29%	9.00%	x	1.45	=	11.15%	+	0.00%
37	1.00%	-$415,801	-$135,420	2007	-23.61%	0.00%	x	1.45	=	0.00%	+	0.00%
38	1.00%	-$410,390	-$115,066	2008	-9.37%	0.00%	x	1.45	=	0.00%	+	0.00%
39	1.00%	-$405,281	-$85,970	2009	7.96%	7.96%	x	1.45	=	11.15%	+	0.00%
40	1.00%	-$445,254	-$46,721	2010	-0.86%	0.00%	x	1.45	=	0.00%	+	0.00%

To make it easier for you to reference my commentary, this is the same ledger as shown in the previous two pages.

Regarding the substantial multiplier charges (column 2), the multi-million dollar question is, *"Are they worth it?"*

Column 5 shows the historical S&P 500 returns each year. The floor and cap are applied, creating the *Pre-Multiplier Index Credit* (column 6), which is then multiplied by the *Multiplier Bonus* (column 7) totaling the *Index Credit w/ Multiplier* (column 8). In some real world *IULs*, there is an additional persistency bonus (column 9). In this example, there is no such bonus. The *Total Index Credit (%)* is depicted in column 10. Depending on the *Total Index Credit (%)* each year, the *Total Index Credits ($)* are determined by multiplying column 10 by the *End-Of-Year Value After Charges Before Credit* (column 14).

10 TOTAL INDEX CREDIT (%)	11 TOTAL INDEX CREDITS ($)	12 TOTAL CHARGES ($)	13 YEAR-END GAIN/LOSS ($)	14 EOY VALUE AFTER CHARGES B4 CREDIT	15 EOY GROSS INDEX ACCUMULATED VALUE	16 EOY INDEX VALUE NET OF NT & EXT LOANS
9.00%	$13,244	($72,850)	($59,606)	$147,150	$160,394	-$23
0.00%	$0	($79,309)	($79,309)	$301,085	$301,085	$117,425
0.00%	$0	($134,592)	($134,592)	$1,046,493	$1,046,493	$218,653
11.15%	$198,050	($150,259)	$47,791	$1,776,234	$1,974,284	$468,848
11.15%	$299,536	($167,860)	$131,676	$2,686,424	$2,985,960	$764,127
0.00%	$0	($191,371)	($191,371)	$3,674,589	$3,674,589	$695,373
9.03%	$392,355	($208,492)	$183,863	$4,346,097	$4,738,453	$952,868
9.59%	$516,567	($230,523)	$286,044	$5,387,930	$5,904,496	$1,257,493
11.15%	$728,074	($254,685)	$473,388	$6,529,811	$7,257,885	$1,687,672
0.00%	$0	($281,893)	($281,893)	$7,855,992	$7,855,992	$1,293,340
5.29%	$406,022	($183,312)	$222,710	$7,672,681	$8,078,702	$771,382
11.15%	$879,660	($189,372)	$690,288	$7,889,330	$8,768,990	$1,110,918
0.03%	$2,245	($199,713)	($197,468)	$8,569,277	$8,571,522	$545,863
11.15%	$933,356	($200,617)	$732,739	$8,370,905	$9,304,261	$893,370
11.15%	$1,013,987	($210,203)	$803,785	$9,094,058	$10,108,046	$1,293,432
11.15%	$1,108,083	($170,078)	$938,006	$9,937,968	$11,046,051	$1,808,336
0.00%	$0	($179,270)	($179,270)	$10,866,782	$10,866,782	$1,185,656
11.15%	$1,192,041	($175,829)	$1,016,212	$10,690,952	$11,882,994	$1,737,174
0.00%	$0	($182,248)	($182,248)	$11,700,745	$11,700,745	$1,067,926
11.15%	$1,285,261	($173,741)	$1,111,520	$11,527,004	$12,812,265	$1,669,071
11.15%	$1,409,209	($173,615)	$1,235,594	$12,638,650	$14,047,859	$2,369,792
11.15%	$1,547,406	($169,777)	$1,377,629	$13,878,082	$15,425,488	$3,186,873
1.19%	$182,132	($175,399)	$6,733	$15,250,089	$15,432,221	$2,375,593
11.15%	$1,700,663	($179,635)	$1,521,028	$15,252,586	$16,953,249	$3,039,343
11.15%	$1,868,056	($199,381)	$1,668,675	$16,753,868	$18,621,924	$3,809,590
11.15%	$2,051,611	($221,829)	$1,829,781	$18,400,095	$20,451,706	$4,697,819
10.67%	$2,156,684	($245,848)	$1,910,835	$20,205,857	$22,362,541	$5,621,908
11.15%	$2,463,151	($271,498)	$2,191,653	$22,091,043	$24,554,194	$6,779,451
11.15%	$2,704,246	($300,870)	$2,403,376	$24,253,324	$26,957,570	$8,099,079
0.00%	$0	($333,382)	($333,382)	$26,624,188	$26,624,188	$6,629,930
0.00%	$0	($340,452)	($340,452)	$26,283,736	$26,283,736	$5,099,193
11.15%	$2,891,829	($348,050)	$2,543,779	$25,935,686	$28,827,515	$6,395,554
11.15%	$3,171,223	($386,051)	$2,785,172	$28,441,464	$31,612,687	$8,103,992
11.15%	$3,477,039	($428,479)	$3,048,560	$31,184,208	$34,661,247	$10,024,135
11.15%	$3,811,691	($475,679)	$3,336,012	$34,185,568	$37,997,259	$12,177,566
11.15%	$4,177,893	($527,369)	$3,650,524	$37,469,890	$41,647,783	$14,588,744
0.00%	$0	($551,221)	($551,221)	$41,096,562	$41,096,562	$12,738,689
0.00%	$0	($525,456)	($525,456)	$40,571,106	$40,571,106	$10,852,055
11.15%	$4,468,904	($491,251)	$3,977,653	$40,079,855	$44,548,759	$13,403,193
0.00%	$0	($491,975)	($491,975)	$44,056,784	$44,056,784	$11,416,231

You will notice that in years wherein the index credit was 0.00%, the *Total Index Credits ($)* column shows a $0 index credit (column 11). You will also notice that in some years, the values in the *Total Index Credits ($)* column (column 11) are greater than the *Total Charges ($)* in column 12, resulting in a *Year-End Gain* (column 13), and in other years, the charges were greater than the credits, resulting in a *Year-End Loss*.

These gains/losses are reflected in the *End-Of-Year Gross Index Account Value* (column 15). The total cumulative third-party lender debt (if any exist in that year) is then backed out of column 15, as is any internal carrier debt balance incurred by any *Participating Loans*, creating an *End-Of-Year Net Index Account Value* (column 16), which is a proxy for the *Policy Cash Value Net Of Loans*.

YEAR	1 3RD PARTY PAYOFF USING PARTICIPATING LOAN	2 INCOME DRAWDOWNS PARTICIPATING LOANS	3 CUMULATIVE ACCRUED INTERNAL LOAN PRINCIPAL	4 ACCRUED INTERNAL LOAN INTEREST	5 INDEX CREDIT AFTER CHARGES
1	$0	$0	$0	$0	$0
2	$0	$0	$0	$0	$0
3	$0	$0	$0	$0	$0
4	$0	$0	$0	$0	$0
5	$0	$0	$0	$0	$0
6	$0	$0	$0	$0	$0
7	$0	$0	$0	$0	$0
8	$0	$0	$0	$0	$0
9	$0	$0	$0	$0	$0
10	$0	$0	$0	$0	$0
11	-$6,972,634	$0	-$6,972,634	-$334,686	$248,529
12	$0	$0	-$7,307,321	-$350,751	$645,257
13	$0	$0	-$7,658,072	-$367,587	$1,440
14	$0	$0	-$8,025,659	-$385,232	$717,417
15	$0	$0	-$8,410,891	-$403,723	$798,073
16	$0	$0	-$8,814,614	-$423,101	$892,291
17	$0	$0	-$9,237,715	-$443,410	$0
18	$0	$0	-$9,681,126	-$464,694	$992,432
19	$0	$0	-$10,145,820	-$486,999	$0
20	$0	$0	-$10,632,819	-$510,375	$1,104,582
21	$0	$0	-$11,143,194	-$534,873	$1,054,420
22	$0	$0	-$11,678,068	-$560,547	$1,368,463
23	$0	-$220,000	-$12,458,615	-$598,014	$141,094
24	$0	-$220,000	-$13,276,628	-$637,278	$1,579,280
25	$0	-$220,000	-$14,133,907	-$678,428	$1,774,723
26	$0	-$220,000	-$15,032,334	-$721,552	$1,991,866
27	$0	-$220,000	-$15,973,886	-$766,747	$1,828,591
28	$0	-$220,000	-$16,960,633	-$814,110	$2,490,907
29	$0	-$220,000	-$17,994,743	-$863,748	$2,787,885
30	$0	-$220,000	-$19,078,491	-$915,768	$0
31	$0	-$220,000	-$20,214,258	-$970,284	$0
32	$0	-$220,000	-$21,404,543	-$1,027,418	$3,154,246
33	$0	$0	-$22,431,961	-$1,076,734	$3,505,413
34	$0	$0	-$23,508,695	-$1,128,417	$3,895,625
35	$0	$0	-$24,637,112	-$1,182,581	$4,190,158
36	$0	$0	-$25,819,694	-$1,239,345	$4,811,195
37	$0	$0	-$27,059,039	-$1,298,834	$0
38	$0	$0	-$28,357,873	-$1,361,178	$0
39	$0	$0	-$29,719,051	-$1,426,514	$4,736,859
40	$0	$0	-$31,145,565	-$1,494,987	$0

The above ledger is different than the one on the previous pages. This one depicts the correlation between the *Participating Loan* debt and the *Index Credits* received in the *Index Account* when opting to pay off the third-party lender using a *Participating Loan*.

Personally, I think it is important to transparently show clients examples wherein their net account value may decrease in a given year due to the internal interest charged on *Participating Loans*, despite the 0.00% floor.

This ledger above shows the $6,972,634 third-party loan being paid off using a *Participating Loan* in year 11 (column 1) plus the $2,200,000 *Cost Recovery* drawdowns (column 2) during the 40-year period that produced the *Worst Compounded Annual Growth Rate* out of 121 different 40-year periods analyzed. The interest charged using a *Participating Loan Rate (PLR)* of 5.00% is

PREMIUM FINANCED LIFE INSURANCE

6 CUMULATIVE INTERNAL DEBT BALANCE	7 CUMULATIVE INDEXED LOAN ACCOUNT VALUE	8 CUMULATIVE PAR LOAN GAIN/LOSS	9 EOY GROSS INDEX ACCUMULATED VALUE	10 EOY INDEX VALUE NET OF INT & EXT LOANS
$0	$0	$0	$160,394	-$23
$0	$0	$0	$301,085	$117,425
$0	$0	$0	$1,046,493	$218,653
$0	$0	$0	$1,974,284	$468,848
$0	$0	$0	$2,985,960	$764,127
$0	$0	$0	$3,674,589	$695,373
$0	$0	$0	$4,738,453	$952,868
$0	$0	$0	$5,904,496	$1,257,493
$0	$0	$0	$7,257,885	$1,687,672
$0	$0	$0	$7,855,992	**$1,293,340**
-$7,307,321	$7,341,611	$34,290	$8,078,702	$771,382
-$7,658,072	$8,160,201	**$502,129**	$8,768,990	$1,110,918
-$8,025,659	$8,162,338	**$136,679**	$8,571,522	$545,863
-$8,410,891	$9,072,439	**$661,548**	$9,304,261	$893,370
-$8,814,614	$10,084,016	**$1,269,402**	$10,108,046	$1,293,432
-$9,237,715	$11,208,383	**$1,970,668**	$11,046,051	$1,808,336
-$9,681,126	$11,208,383	**$1,527,258**	$10,866,782	$1,185,656
-$10,145,820	$12,458,118	**$2,312,298**	$11,882,994	$1,737,174
-$10,632,819	$12,458,118	**$1,825,299**	$11,700,745	$1,067,926
-$11,143,194	$13,847,198	**$2,704,004**	$12,812,265	**$1,669,071**
-$11,678,068	$15,391,161	**$3,713,093**	$14,047,859	$2,369,792
-$12,238,615	$17,107,275	**$4,868,660**	$15,425,488	$3,186,873
-$13,056,628	$17,534,215	**$4,477,586**	$15,432,221	$2,375,593
-$13,913,907	$19,733,810	**$5,819,903**	$16,953,249	$3,039,343
-$14,812,334	$22,178,660	**$7,366,326**	$18,621,924	$3,809,590
-$15,753,886	$24,896,110	**$9,142,224**	$20,451,706	$4,697,819
-$16,740,633	$27,796,893	**$11,056,260**	$22,362,541	$5,621,908
-$17,774,743	$31,140,776	**$13,366,033**	$24,554,194	$6,779,451
-$18,858,491	$34,857,503	**$15,999,012**	$26,957,570	$8,099,079
-$19,994,258	$35,077,503	**$15,083,244**	$26,624,188	**$6,629,930**
-$21,184,543	$35,297,503	**$14,112,960**	$26,283,736	$5,099,193
-$22,431,961	$39,477,704	**$17,045,743**	$28,827,515	$6,395,554
-$23,508,695	$43,879,468	**$20,370,773**	$31,612,687	$8,103,992
-$24,637,112	$48,772,029	**$24,134,917**	$34,661,247	$10,024,135
-$25,819,694	$54,210,110	**$28,390,417**	$37,997,259	$12,177,566
-$27,059,039	$60,254,537	**$33,195,498**	$41,647,783	$14,588,744
-$28,357,873	$60,254,537	**$31,896,665**	$41,096,562	$12,738,689
-$29,719,051	$60,254,537	**$30,535,487**	$40,571,106	$10,852,055
-$31,145,565	$66,972,918	**$35,827,353**	$44,548,759	$13,403,193
-$32,640,552	$66,972,918	**$34,332,366**	$44,056,784	**$11,416,231**

accrued (column 4) and rolled into the *Cumulative Accrued Internal Loan Principal* (column 3).

The $6,972,634 (column 1) and $2,200,000 (column 2) is credited using the same S&P 500-correlated floor/cap index crediting method, receiving a positive index credit during years when the S&P 500 generates a positive return, and credits $0 during years wherein the S&P 500 produces a negative return (column 5).

The *Cumulative Internal Debt Balance* is depicted in column 6, and the *Cumulative Index Balance On Participating Loans* is depicted in column 7, producing a *Cumulative Loan Gain/Loss* in column 8.

Due to using *Participating Loans* to payoff the third-party lender in year 15 and to execute the *Cost Recovery* drawdowns in years 23-32, the cumulative internal debt totals a negative $32,640,552 by year 40 (bottom of column 6).

However, the cumulative gains in the separate index account total $66,972,918 (bottom of column 7), resulting in a net gain of $34,332,366 in year 40 (bottom of column 8) due to the *Participating Loan* arrangement during the 40-Year period with the *Worst Compounded Annual Growth Rate* out of 121 different 40-year periods analyzed.

This is extremely impressive given this was a terrible 40-year sequence, yet the *Participating Loan* proposition still netted a $34,332,366 positive arbitrage/gain.

Every client should see this type of backtested scenario when considering *Premium Financed Life Insurance* as an estate planning strategy. Without this backtesting analyzation, how would any know if this proposition would stand up during times of volatility?

Being able to show a client this type of modeling is invaluable because it shows that a tremendous effort was made in the areas of:

1. Full Transparency.
2. Client Education.
3. Consumer Protection.
4. Explaining How Volatility Can Produce a Range of Different Potential Outcomes.
5. Explaining The Relationship Between Credits and Charges.

Chapter 9
Estate Planning & Life Insurance

When it comes to estate tax planning, wealthy clients essentially have two options:

1. Do nothing and give away 40% of their wealth to the government in the form of estate taxes, or…
2. Use life insurance to pay the estate taxes for them.

Making the decision to buy life insurance should be based on one simple mathematical equation:

If the money you would have spent on life insurance can be invested in an alternative asset, and that asset value (after 40.00% estate taxes) becomes greater than the tax-free death benefit of the life insurance policy, then you should NOT buy the life insurance policy. But if 60% of that alternative asset value is less valuable than the net death benefit, then you SHOULD buy the life insurance. It really is that simple.

I will model this alternative asset (which I will refer to as a *Hypothetical Equities & Bonds Account*) and calculate its value after the 40% estate tax due.

I will then compare it to the *Premium Financed IUL Proxy* during the 40-year S&P 500 historical period that produced the *Best Compounded Annual Growth Rate* of the 121 different 40-year periods analyzed, AND ALSO during the 40-year S&P 500 historical period that produced the *Worst Compounded Annual Growth Rate* of the 121 different 40-year periods analyzed.

HYPOTHETICAL EQUITIES & BONDS ACCOUNT vs. LEVERAGED H
WORST PRE-PANDEMIC CAGR 40-YEAR PERIOD OUT OF 121 DIFFERENT IN

	EQUITIES	BONDS	Current Adjusted Gross Income (AGI):	$250,000	%
<AGE 56:	70.00%	30.00%	Current Income Tax Rate:	37.10%	%
AGE 56+:	70.00%	30.00%	Long-Term Capital Gains Tax Rate:	28.10%	%
			State of Residence:	CA	

# YEAR	AGE	1 ANNUAL INVESTED	2 CALENDAR YEAR	3 GROSS EQUITIES RETURN	4 AFTER-FEE EQUITIES RETURN	5 AFTER-FEE & TAX EQUITIES RETURN	6 CALENDAR YEAR	7 GROSS BOND RETURN	8 AFTER-FEE BOND RETURN
1	50	$144,000	1971	14.42%	13.07%	9.39%	1971	5.27%	3.92%
2	51	$292,061	1972	0.08%	-1.27%	-1.27%	1972	-0.44%	-1.79%
3	52	$444,314	1973	-39.40%	-40.75%	-40.75%	1973	-2.37%	-3.72%
4	53	$600,895	1974	34.00%	32.65%	23.47%	1974	-8.16%	-9.51%
5	54	$761,943	1975	27.48%	26.13%	18.79%	1975	-5.07%	-6.42%
6	55	$927,601	1976	-6.28%	-7.63%	-7.63%	1976	9.68%	8.33%
7	56	$1,098,017	1977	8.23%	6.88%	4.94%	1977	-4.89%	-6.24%
8	57	$1,114,174	1978	8.61%	7.26%	5.22%	1978	-7.81%	-9.16%
9	58	$1,130,680	1979	16.76%	15.41%	11.08%	1979	-9.51%	-10.86%
10	59	$1,147,543	1980	-5.40%	-6.75%	-6.75%	1980	-14.57%	-15.92%
11	60	$0	1981	5.65%	4.30%	3.09%	1981	-1.94%	-3.29%
12	61	$0	1982	39.91%	38.56%	27.72%	1982	25.14%	23.79%
13	62	$0	1983	2.02%	0.67%	0.48%	1983	-0.01%	-1.36%
14	63	$0	1984	11.62%	10.27%	7.38%	1984	9.04%	7.69%
15	64	$0	1985	29.04%	27.69%	19.91%	1985	21.41%	20.06%
16	65	$0	1986	41.13%	39.78%	28.60%	1986	21.97%	20.62%
17	66	$0	1987	-13.51%	-14.86%	-14.86%	1987	-8.32%	-9.67%
18	67	$0	1988	30.41%	29.06%	20.89%	1988	3.98%	2.63%
19	68	$0	1989	-10.34%	-11.69%	-11.69%	1989	12.27%	10.92%
20	69	$0	1990	28.73%	27.38%	19.69%	1990	0.79%	-0.56%
21	70	$0	1991	9.72%	8.37%	6.02%	1991	10.33%	8.98%
22	71	$0	1992	11.84%	10.49%	7.55%	1992	6.15%	4.80%
23	72	$0	1993	2.82%	1.47%	1.06%	1993	10.94%	9.59%
24	73	$0	1994	28.30%	26.95%	19.38%	1994	-10.37%	-11.72%
25	74	$0	1995	19.61%	18.26%	13.13%	1995	20.11%	18.76%
26	75	$0	1996	39.82%	38.47%	27.66%	1996	-1.46%	-2.81%
27	76	$0	1997	9.36%	8.01%	5.76%	1997	7.43%	6.08%
28	77	$0	1998	28.13%	26.78%	19.25%	1998	13.16%	11.81%
29	78	$0	1999	13.99%	12.64%	9.09%	1999	-10.22%	-11.57%
30	79	$0	2000	-25.54%	-26.89%	-26.89%	2000	12.84%	11.49%
31	80	$0	2001	-19.68%	-21.03%	-21.03%	2001	2.67%	1.32%
32	81	$0	2002	24.16%	22.81%	16.40%	2002	13.32%	11.97%
33	82	$0	2003	13.91%	12.56%	9.03%	2003	-1.85%	-3.20%
34	83	$0	2004	12.25%	10.90%	7.84%	2004	1.77%	0.42%
35	84	$0	2005	10.71%	9.36%	6.73%	2005	-0.51%	-1.86%
36	85	$0	2006	16.29%	14.94%	10.74%	2006	-1.23%	-2.58%
37	86	$0	2007	-21.61%	-22.96%	-22.96%	2007	7.15%	5.80%
38	87	$0	2008	-7.37%	-8.72%	-8.72%	2008	15.66%	14.31%
39	88	$0	2009	9.96%	8.61%	6.19%	2009	-10.80%	-12.15%
40	89	$0	2010	1.14%	-0.21%	-0.21%	2010	6.71%	5.36%
		Average Equities Return:		10.02%			Average T-Bond Return:	3.46%	Avera

The deposits into this *Hypothetical Equities & Bonds Account* are equal to the illustrated interest payments in the premium financed life insurance policy (column 1). In this depiction, 70% of the portfolio uses historical S&P 500 returns plus an additional 2.00% bonus added as a hypothetical S&P 500 dividend, and 30% of the portfolio uses historical 10-year T-Bond returns.

PREMIUM FINANCED LIFE INSURANCE

HYPOTHETICAL SYNTHETIC ASSET (LHSA)

INDEX PERIODS ANALYZED (STARTING 10/1/1971)

of Equities Taxed at STCG Tax Rates:	0.00%
of Equities Taxed at LTCG Tax Rates:	100.00%
of Bonds Taxed at STCG Tax Rates:	100.00%
Estate Tax Rates:	40.00%

Advisor Fee:	0.50%
Fund Manager Fee:	0.70%
Broker Dealer Fee:	0.15%
Investment Fees (All-In):	**1.35%**

9 AFTER-FEE & TAX BOND RETURN	1 TOTAL CHARGES	11 NET RETURN	12 INCOME DRAWDOWNS	13 AFTER-TAX ACCOUNT VALUE		14 AFTER-ESTATE TAX ACCOUNT VALUE		15 GREATER OF DB & LHSA ACCOUNT VALUE	16 LHSA INCREASE
2.46%	1.35%	7.32%	$0	$154,534	=	$92,721	vs	$25,925,824	27861.24%
-1.79%	1.35%	-1.42%	$0	$440,235	=	$264,141	vs	$25,792,778	9664.78%
-3.72%	1.35%	-29.64%	$0	$622,353	=	$373,412	vs	$25,762,750	6799.29%
-9.51%	1.35%	13.58%	$0	$1,389,321	=	$833,593	vs	$25,841,729	3000.04%
-6.42%	1.35%	11.22%	$0	$2,392,721	=	$1,435,633	vs	$26,035,434	1713.52%
5.24%	1.35%	-3.77%	$0	$3,195,282	=	$1,917,169	vs	$26,349,622	1274.40%
-6.24%	1.35%	1.59%	$0	$4,361,461	=	$2,616,877	vs	$26,791,285	923.79%
-9.16%	1.35%	0.91%	$0	$5,525,259	=	$3,315,156	vs	$21,415,885	546.00%
-10.86%	1.35%	4.50%	$0	$6,955,385	=	$4,173,231	vs	$21,415,885	413.17%
-15.92%	1.35%	-9.50%	$0	$7,333,362	=	**$4,400,017**	vs	**$21,415,885**	386.72%
-3.29%	1.35%	1.18%	$0	$7,419,771	=	$4,451,863	vs	$20,729,885	365.65%
14.96%	1.35%	23.90%	$0	$9,192,815	=	$5,515,689	vs	$20,010,271	262.79%
-1.36%	1.35%	-0.07%	$0	$9,186,167	=	$5,511,700	vs	$19,255,396	249.35%
4.84%	1.35%	6.62%	$0	$9,794,391	=	$5,876,635	vs	$18,463,532	214.19%
12.62%	1.35%	17.72%	$0	$11,530,234	=	$6,918,140	vs	$17,632,867	154.88%
12.97%	1.35%	23.91%	$0	$14,287,218	=	$8,572,331	vs	$16,761,499	95.53%
-9.67%	1.35%	-13.30%	$0	$12,386,453	=	$7,431,872	vs	$15,847,434	113.24%
1.66%	1.35%	15.12%	$0	$14,259,413	=	$8,555,648	vs	$14,888,580	74.02%
6.87%	1.35%	-6.12%	$0	$13,386,082	=	$8,031,649	vs	$13,882,742	72.85%
-0.56%	1.35%	13.61%	$0	$15,208,487	=	**$9,125,092**	vs	**$12,827,618**	40.58%
5.65%	1.35%	5.91%	$0	$16,106,877	=	$9,664,126	vs	$11,720,793	21.28%
3.02%	1.35%	6.19%	$0	$17,103,404	=	$10,262,043	vs	$10,578,497	3.08%
6.03%	1.35%	2.55%	$0	$17,539,654	=	$10,523,793	vs	$10,690,715	1.59%
-11.72%	1.35%	10.05%	$0	$19,301,976	=	$11,581,186	vs	$10,790,801	-6.82%
11.80%	1.35%	12.73%	$0	$21,759,302	=	$13,055,581	vs	$11,316,636	-13.32%
-2.81%	1.35%	18.52%	-$766,123	$24,880,936	=	$14,928,562	vs	$13,071,657	-12.44%
3.82%	1.35%	5.18%	-$766,123	$25,363,684	=	$15,218,210	vs	$13,938,274	-8.41%
7.43%	1.35%	15.71%	-$766,123	$28,460,758	=	$17,076,455	vs	$16,176,198	-5.27%
-11.57%	1.35%	2.89%	-$766,123	$28,495,353	=	$17,097,212	vs	$18,755,629	9.70%
7.23%	1.35%	-16.65%	-$766,123	$23,111,821	=	**$13,867,093**	vs	**$15,960,647**	15.10%
0.83%	1.35%	-14.47%	-$766,123	$19,112,108	=	$11,467,265	vs	$13,019,986	13.54%
7.53%	1.35%	13.74%	-$766,123	$20,866,783	=	$12,520,070	vs	$15,666,888	25.13%
-3.20%	1.35%	5.36%	-$766,123	$21,178,081	=	$12,706,848	vs	$18,713,933	47.27%
0.26%	1.35%	5.56%	-$766,123	$21,547,649	=	$12,928,589	vs	$22,205,756	71.76%
-1.86%	1.35%	4.15%	-$766,123	$21,644,775	=	$12,986,865	vs	$25,210,348	94.12%
-2.58%	1.35%	6.75%	$0	$23,105,136	=	$13,863,082	vs	$30,450,132	119.65%
3.65%	1.35%	-14.97%	$0	$19,645,496	=	$11,787,297	vs	$27,259,254	131.26%
9.00%	1.35%	-3.40%	$0	$18,976,949	=	$11,386,170	vs	$23,886,278	109.78%
-12.15%	1.35%	0.69%	$0	$19,107,402	=	$11,464,441	vs	$27,501,818	139.89%
3.37%	1.35%	0.87%	$0	$19,273,077	=	**$11,563,846**	vs	**$23,729,913**	105.21%

Average Net Portfolio Return: 3.62%

WORST 40

The all-in investment fee in this model is 1.35%, which assumes a 0.50% advisor fee, a 0.70% fund manager fee, and a 0.15% broker dealer fee. The S&P gains are taxed at 37.00% and the 10-year T-Bonds are only taxed at 28.10%. And finally, the account balance is taxed at 40.00% upon generational transfer to represent estate taxes.

HYPOTHETICAL EQUITIES & BONDS ACCOUNT vs. LEVERAGED H
WORST PRE-PANDEMIC CAGR 40-YEAR PERIOD OUT OF 121 DIFFERENT IN

	EQUITIES	BONDS	Current Adjusted Gross Income (AGI):	$250,000	%
<AGE 56:	70.00%	30.00%	Current Income Tax Rate:	37.10%	%
AGE 56+:	70.00%	30.00%	Long-Term Capital Gains Tax Rate:	28.10%	%
			State of Residence:	CA	

#		1	2	3	4	5	6	7	8
YEAR	AGE	ANNUAL INVESTED	CALENDAR YEAR	GROSS EQUITIES RETURN	AFTER-FEE EQUITIES RETURN	AFTER-FEE & TAX EQUITIES RETURN	CALENDAR YEAR	GROSS BOND RETURN	AFTER-FEE BOND RETURN
1	50	$144,000	1971	14.42%	13.07%	9.39%	1971	5.27%	3.92%
2	51	$292,061	1972	0.08%	-1.27%	-1.27%	1972	-0.44%	-1.79%
3	52	$444,314	1973	-39.40%	-40.75%	-40.75%	1973	-2.37%	-3.72%
4	53	$600,895	1974	34.00%	32.65%	23.47%	1974	-8.16%	-9.51%
5	54	$761,943	1975	27.48%	26.13%	18.79%	1975	-5.07%	-6.42%
6	55	$927,601	1976	-6.28%	-7.63%	-7.63%	1976	9.68%	8.33%
7	56	$1,098,017	1977	8.23%	6.88%	4.94%	1977	-4.89%	-6.24%
8	57	$1,114,174	1978	8.61%	7.26%	5.22%	1978	-7.81%	-9.16%
9	58	$1,130,680	1979	16.76%	15.41%	11.08%	1979	-9.51%	-10.86%
10	59	$1,147,543	1980	-5.40%	-6.75%	-6.75%	1980	-14.57%	-15.92%
11	60	$0	1981	5.65%	4.30%	3.09%	1981	-1.94%	-3.29%
12	61	$0	1982	39.91%	38.56%	27.72%	1982	25.14%	23.79%
13	62	$0	1983	2.02%	0.67%	0.48%	1983	-0.01%	-1.36%
14	63	$0	1984	11.62%	10.27%	7.38%	1984	9.04%	7.69%
15	64	$0	1985	29.04%	27.69%	19.91%	1985	21.41%	20.06%
16	65	$0	1986	41.13%	39.78%	28.60%	1986	21.97%	20.62%
17	66	$0	1987	-13.51%	-14.86%	-14.86%	1987	-8.32%	-9.67%
18	67	$0	1988	30.41%	29.06%	20.89%	1988	3.98%	2.63%
19	68	$0	1989	-10.34%	-11.69%	-11.69%	1989	12.27%	10.92%
20	69	$0	1990	28.73%	27.38%	19.69%	1990	0.79%	-0.56%
21	70	$0	1991	9.72%	8.37%	6.02%	1991	10.33%	8.98%
22	71	$0	1992	11.84%	10.49%	7.55%	1992	6.15%	4.80%
23	72	$0	1993	2.82%	1.47%	1.06%	1993	10.94%	9.59%
24	73	$0	1994	28.30%	26.95%	19.38%	1994	-10.37%	-11.72%
25	74	$0	1995	19.61%	18.26%	13.13%	1995	20.11%	18.76%
26	75	$0	1996	39.82%	38.47%	27.66%	1996	-1.46%	-2.81%
27	76	$0	1997	9.36%	8.01%	5.76%	1997	7.43%	6.08%
28	77	$0	1998	28.13%	26.78%	19.25%	1998	13.16%	11.81%
29	78	$0	1999	13.99%	12.64%	9.09%	1999	-10.22%	-11.57%
30	79	$0	2000	-25.54%	-26.89%	-26.89%	2000	12.84%	11.49%
31	80	$0	2001	-19.68%	-21.03%	-21.03%	2001	2.67%	1.32%
32	81	$0	2002	24.16%	22.81%	16.40%	2002	13.32%	11.97%
33	82	$0	2003	13.91%	12.56%	9.03%	2003	-1.85%	-3.20%
34	83	$0	2004	12.25%	10.90%	7.84%	2004	1.77%	0.42%
35	84	$0	2005	10.71%	9.36%	6.73%	2005	-0.51%	-1.86%
36	85	$0	2006	16.29%	14.94%	10.74%	2006	-1.23%	-2.58%
37	86	$0	2007	-21.61%	-22.96%	-22.96%	2007	7.15%	5.80%
38	87	$0	2008	-7.37%	-8.72%	-8.72%	2008	15.66%	14.31%
39	88	$0	2009	9.96%	8.61%	6.19%	2009	-10.80%	-12.15%
40	89	$0	2010	1.14%	-0.21%	-0.21%	2010	6.71%	5.36%
		Average Equities Return:		10.02%			Average T-Bond Return:	3.46%	Avera

To make it easier for you to reference the ledger while reading my commentary, I will repeat the above ledger in the following pages. The purpose of this model is to compare the value of this *Hypothetical Equities & Bonds Account* to the *Premium Financed IUL Proxy*. In column 15, I have taken the greater of *The Proxy's Net Account Value* and the *As-Illustrated Death Benefit* (as depicted in the carrier illustration).

PREMIUM FINANCED LIFE INSURANCE

HYPOTHETICAL SYNTHETIC ASSET (LHSA)

INDEX PERIODS ANALYZED (STARTING 10/1/1971)

AGE 22

of Equities Taxed at STCG Tax Rates:	0.00%				Advisor Fee:	0.50%
of Equities Taxed at LTCG Tax Rates:	100.00%				Fund Manager Fee:	0.70%
of Bonds Taxed at STCG Tax Rates:	100.00%				Broker Dealer Fee:	0.15%
Estate Tax Rates:	40.00%				Investment Fees (All-In):	1.35%

9 AFTER-FEE & TAX BOND RETURN	10 TOTAL CHARGES	11 NET RETURN	12 INCOME DRAWDOWNS	13 AFTER-TAX ACCOUNT VALUE		14 AFTER-ESTATE TAX ACCOUNT VALUE		15 GREATER OF DB & LHSA ACCOUNT VALUE	16 LHSA INCREASE
2.46%	1.35%	7.32%	$0	$154,534	=	$92,721	vs	$25,925,824	27861.24%
-1.79%	1.35%	-1.42%	$0	$440,235	=	$264,141	vs	$25,792,778	9664.78%
-3.72%	1.35%	-29.64%	$0	$622,353	=	$373,412	vs	$25,762,750	6799.29%
-9.51%	1.35%	13.58%	$0	$1,389,321	=	$833,593	vs	$25,841,729	3000.04%
-6.42%	1.35%	11.22%	$0	$2,392,721	=	$1,435,633	vs	$26,035,434	1713.52%
5.24%	1.35%	-3.77%	$0	$3,195,282	=	$1,917,169	vs	$26,349,622	1274.40%
-6.24%	1.35%	1.59%	$0	$4,361,461	=	$2,616,877	vs	$26,791,285	923.79%
-9.16%	1.35%	0.91%	$0	$5,525,259	=	$3,315,156	vs	$21,415,885	546.00%
-10.86%	1.35%	4.50%	$0	$6,955,385	=	$4,173,231	vs	$21,415,885	413.17%
-15.92%	1.35%	-9.50%	$0	$7,333,362	=	**$4,400,017**	vs	**$21,415,885**	386.72%
-3.29%	1.35%	1.18%	$0	$7,419,771	=	$4,451,863	vs	$20,729,885	365.65%
14.96%	1.35%	23.90%	$0	$9,192,815	=	$5,515,689	vs	$20,010,271	262.79%
-1.36%	1.35%	-0.07%	$0	$9,186,167	=	$5,511,700	vs	$19,255,396	249.35%
4.84%	1.35%	6.62%	$0	$9,794,391	=	$5,876,635	vs	$18,463,532	214.19%
12.62%	1.35%	17.72%	$0	$11,530,234	=	$6,918,140	vs	$17,632,867	154.88%
12.97%	1.35%	23.91%	$0	$14,287,218	=	$8,572,331	vs	$16,761,499	95.53%
-9.67%	1.35%	-13.30%	$0	$12,386,453	=	$7,431,872	vs	$15,847,434	113.24%
1.66%	1.35%	15.12%	$0	$14,259,413	=	$8,555,648	vs	$14,888,580	74.02%
6.87%	1.35%	-6.12%	$0	$13,386,082	=	$8,031,649	vs	$13,882,742	72.85%
-0.56%	1.35%	13.61%	$0	$15,208,487	=	**$9,125,092**	vs	**$12,827,618**	40.58%
5.65%	1.35%	5.91%	$0	$16,106,877	=	$9,664,126	vs	$11,720,793	21.28%
3.02%	1.35%	6.19%	$0	$17,103,404	=	$10,262,043	vs	$10,578,497	3.08%
6.03%	1.35%	2.55%	$0	$17,539,654	=	$10,523,793	vs	$10,690,715	1.59%
-11.72%	1.35%	10.05%	$0	$19,301,976	=	$11,581,186	vs	$10,790,801	-6.82%
11.80%	1.35%	12.73%	$0	$21,759,302	=	$13,055,581	vs	$11,316,636	-13.32%
-2.81%	1.35%	18.52%	-$766,123	$24,880,936	=	$14,928,562	vs	$13,071,657	-12.44%
3.82%	1.35%	5.18%	-$766,123	$25,363,684	=	$15,218,210	vs	$13,938,274	-8.41%
7.43%	1.35%	15.71%	-$766,123	$28,460,758	=	$17,076,455	vs	$16,176,198	-5.27%
-11.57%	1.35%	2.89%	-$766,123	$28,495,353	=	$17,097,212	vs	$18,755,629	9.70%
7.23%	1.35%	-16.65%	-$766,123	$23,111,821	=	**$13,867,093**	vs	**$15,960,647**	15.10%
0.83%	1.35%	-14.47%	-$766,123	$19,112,108	=	$11,467,265	vs	$13,019,986	13.54%
7.53%	1.35%	13.74%	-$766,123	$20,866,783	=	$12,520,070	vs	$15,666,888	25.13%
-3.20%	1.35%	5.36%	-$766,123	$21,178,081	=	$12,706,848	vs	$18,713,933	47.27%
0.26%	1.35%	5.56%	-$766,123	$21,547,649	=	$12,928,589	vs	$22,205,756	71.76%
-1.86%	1.35%	4.15%	-$766,123	$21,644,775	=	$12,986,865	vs	$25,210,348	94.12%
-2.58%	1.35%	6.75%	$0	$23,105,136	=	$13,863,082	vs	$30,450,132	119.65%
3.65%	1.35%	-14.97%	$0	$19,645,496	=	$11,787,297	vs	$27,259,254	131.26%
9.00%	1.35%	-3.40%	$0	$18,976,949	=	$11,386,170	vs	$23,886,278	109.78%
-12.15%	1.35%	0.69%	$0	$19,107,402	=	$11,464,441	vs	$27,501,818	139.89%
3.37%	1.35%	0.87%	$0	$19,273,077	=	**$11,563,846**	vs	**$23,729,913**	105.21%

Average Net Portfolio Return: 3.62%

WORST 40

Column 16 shows the greater-or-less-than percentage return over/under the *Hypothetical Equities & Bonds Account*. In years 24-28, the ROI is slightly less than the *Hypothetical Equities & Bonds Account*, however in all other years, the *Premium Financed IUL Proxy* drastically outperforms the alternative even during the *Worst 40-Year Period.*

These graphs below depict the greater of the as-illustrated death benefit in the carrier illustration and the net account values of the *Premium Financed IUL Proxy* (because we do not attempt to estimate death benefit amounts in these synthetic proxies), compared to the *Equities & Bonds* account. For the large majority of these 40-year periods, the results aren't even close.

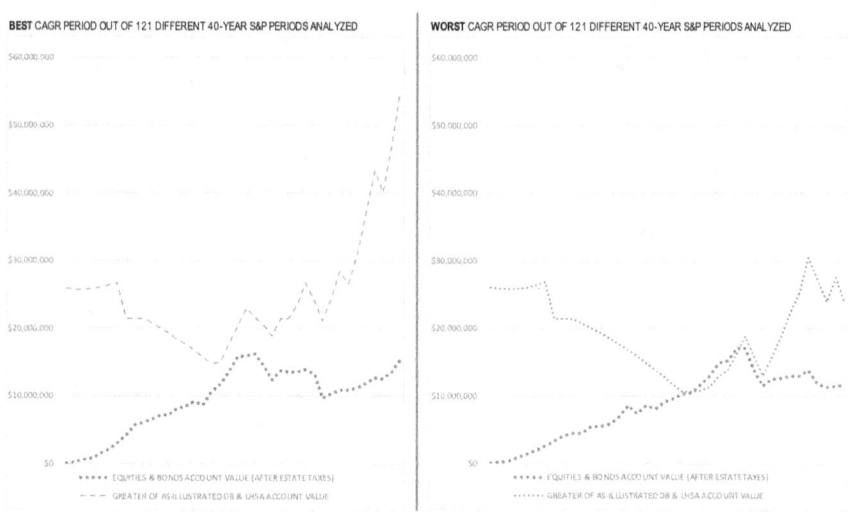

Despite the indisputable math we have just reviewed, there is certainly an emotionally-driven population that feels like they are leaving enough assets behind for *Generation Two (G2)* and don't feel the need to purchase life insurance. Perhaps they have even said, *"No one ever left me an inheritance. My kids are lucky to get whatever I leave them."*

As I said earlier in this chapter, wealthy parents are either going to leave the money to their kids, a charity, or *Uncle Sam*. Even if they don't want to make their kids overly wealthy, I have yet to meet a wealthy individual that prefers the IRS over their favorite charity.

The problem that many wealthy families face is that if the majority of the estate's value is *not* liquid (e.g. real estate value, business valuation, etc.), *Generation Two (G2)* would have to sell the estate's assets to come up with the cash to pay the estate taxes due, and they only have nine months to make this payment.

The IRS does however have an option to finance the estate taxes due. According to IRC Section 6166, *G2* may defer payment of estate taxes if 35%+ of the deceased person's estate is a closely held business. *G2* can pay interest-only in years 1-5 on the estate taxes due, then they can pay principle plus interest amortized over years 6-10. If *G2* defaults on this IRS loan, the IRS can seize and sell the asset.

An advisor once told me about one of his clients wherein the estate was worth $114,000,000 at the time of the second parent's death in 2006. At that time, the estate tax exemption for a married couple was only $4,000,000 (instead of the current $28,394,686 per couple in 2024) and the estate tax rate was 46% (instead of the current 40%). The family's business was in the real estate industry. *G2* elected the 6166 option because they didn't have the liquidity to pay the $50 million in estate taxes due.

Two years later in 2008, the estate/business value plummeted from $114,000,000 to only $54,000,000. *G2's* income plummeted as well, and they defaulted on the 6166 loan.

The IRS seized the estate's assets and sold them for their new fair market value of $54,000,000. However this reduction in estate valuation did not affect the $50,000,000 in estate taxes still due. You see, the estate taxes were calculated based on the value of the estate at the time of death, regardless of the plummeted value two years later.

Ultimately, *G2* was left with only $4,000,000 after they inherited a $114 million estate from their parents.

In this scenario, had there been a $50,000,000 life insurance policy in an *ILIT (Irrevocable Life Insurance Trust)* outside the estate) to pay the future estate tax liability, *G2* could have inherited the entire estate, undiluted by estate taxes.

In the upcoming chapters, we will evaluate several different ways of financing life insurance premiums.

When wealthy parents pass away, it can drive huge wedges between siblings if the estate plan is not well designed and/or clearly delineated. When siblings argue over who gets to keep certain sentimental assets (like the family home and the family business), versus what assets need to be sold in order to pay the estate taxes, it can absolutely destroy a family.

This is why providing liquidity in their time of need is so important, and typically, *Premium Financed Life Insurance* is the most prudent and tax-efficient way to provide such liquidity.

Though it is clearly important to understand the client's financial position when developing an estate plan, the single-most important thing for an advisor to understand is how to identify the difference between what a client *says* they want today, versus how they will *feel* in the future if their personal financial situation does not meet their aspirations.

This can be a challenging truth to uncover – one that takes a tremendous amount of psychological, sociological, and emotional intuitiveness on behalf of the advisor. It also takes a high level of understanding the inter-family relationship dynamics and family governance (or lack thereof).

Here's an example to illustrate what I mean by this.

Let's say you have a wealthy family with a taxable estate value of $100 million. When the patriarch and matriarch both pass away, as of 2024, their heirs will owe $40 million in estate taxes within nine months of their passing. If the majority of the estate value is held in illiquid assets (e.g., Real Estate, Company Valuation, etc.), the adult kids will be forced to sell assets to come up with the cash to pay the 40% in estate taxes.

In this hypothetical example, the eldest son is running the family business and does not want to sell any shares of the business to pay the estate taxes – the family business is his *baby*. The youngest son is living on the family yacht in Miami, living the *playboy* lifestyle, and certainly doesn't want to sell the yacht and the penthouse to pay the estate taxes. The daughter is resentful that she was not chosen to run the family business, and she has a sentimental attachment to the family vacation house in the Hamptons where they spent their summers growing up, and she doesn't want to sell it to pay the estate taxes. Of course, each respective sibling could care less about the assets their other siblings care about, and these disagreements over which assets to liquidate in order to pay the $40 million in estate taxes can absolutely destroy the relationships between siblings.

If there are spouses, children, and grandchildren involved, this can make these family disputes even more volatile. <u>You see, it's not *just* the financial elements that are important. The emotional/relationship dynamics are also important – perhaps even more important.</u>

This is where *Premium Financed Life Insurance* can be such a valuable tool in regards to estate planning and family governance. Assets can be split amongst the surviving siblings based on their preference and emotional attachments, and the life insurance death benefit can take care of the estate taxes due, keeping the peace.

When people ask me what I do for a living, I now say, *"When wealth is transferred from one generation to the next, I make sure the adult kids don't kill each other."*

This response often times leads to some pretty interesting cocktail party discussions without me even trying to solicit my services. You would be amazed that despite how much I try to avoid talking about what I do for a living in social settings, people are fascinated by this topic of inter-family relationship dynamics, especially amongst uber wealthy families.

Chapter 10
First-Dollar Financing (FDF)

Despite the limitations and inaccuracies of carrier illustrations, the client must be shown the carrier illustration for compliance purposes. Contractually speaking, this is what they are accepting when they purchase the policy – not the outcome, but the depiction of the outcome that represents one of many possible outcomes.

In this chapter, I will evaluate the carrier *as-illustrated* outcomes using a real-world *Premium Financed IUL*, using one of several different loan models I have in my design arsenal. It is called First-Dollar Financing (FDF). I am going to assume a static index credit of 5.40%. I will also assume a third-party lender payoff in policy year 11 using a *Participating Loan*.

The third-party lender rate I will use in this case study starts at 7.20% and artificially increases 100bps in year 10 to 8.20%. Future borrowing rates could be greater or less than what is depicted in this case study, and at the time these numbers were run, the most recently published forward curve rates (November 2023) showed a year-two interest rate of only 6.12% (1-Year CMT + 1.85%).

Despite what the forward curve rates may predict, I still chose to artificially increase the borrowing rates each year, just to be overly conservative (which is *not* what my competitors do).

It is also important to note that the client's age and health rating are significant factors that determine the efficiency of *Premium Financed Life Insurance*, for they dictate certain charges within the policy (e.g., mortality cost, cost of insurance, etc.).

The older and unhealthier the client, the less favorable the economics of premium financing become, and if too unfavorable, I am the first one to advise the client to *not* enter a premium financing arrangement.

In this case study, I am assuming the client is a male, age 50, rated as a *Preferred Non-Smoker*.

SUMMARY OF CARRIER-ILLUSTRATED STATIC RETURNS (DESIGNED)
FIRST-DOLLAR FINANCING

Health Rating: **PREFERRED**   Third Party Loan Payoff Type: **PAR LOAN**

YEAR	AGE	1 TOTAL POLICY PREMIUMS	2 EQUITY PREMIUMS	3 BORROWED PREMIUMS	4 CUMULATIVE PF LOAN BALANCE	5 FINANCING INTEREST RATE	6 INTEREST DUE	7 INTEREST ACCRUED	8 CLIENT CONTRIBUTION
1	50	$2,000,000	$0	$2,000,000	$2,000,000	7.20%	$144,000	$0	$144,000
2	51	$2,000,000	$0	$2,000,000	$4,000,000	7.30%	$292,061	$0	$292,061
3	52	$2,000,000	$0	$2,000,000	$6,000,000	7.41%	$444,314	$0	$444,314
4	53	$2,000,000	$0	$2,000,000	$8,000,000	7.51%	$600,895	$0	$600,895
5	54	$2,000,000	$0	$2,000,000	$10,000,000	7.62%	$761,943	$0	$761,943
6	55	$2,000,000	$0	$2,000,000	$12,000,000	7.73%	$927,601	$0	$927,601
7	56	$2,000,000	$0	$2,000,000	$14,000,000	7.84%	$1,098,017	$0	$1,098,017
8	57	$0	$0	$0	$14,000,000	7.96%	$1,114,174	$0	$1,114,174
9	58	$0	$0	$0	$14,000,000	8.08%	$1,130,680	$0	$1,130,680
10	59	$0	$0	$0	$14,000,000	8.20%	$1,147,543	$0	$1,147,543
11	60	$0	$0	$0	$0	0.00%	$0	$0	$0
12	61	$0	$0	$0	$0	0.00%	$0	$0	$0
13	62	$0	$0	$0	$0	0.00%	$0	$0	$0
14	63	$0	$0	$0	$0	0.00%	$0	$0	$0
15	64	$0	$0	$0	$0	0.00%	$0	$0	$0
16	65	$0	$0	$0	$0	0.00%	$0	$0	$0
17	66	$0	$0	$0	$0	0.00%	$0	$0	$0
18	67	$0	$0	$0	$0	0.00%	$0	$0	$0
19	68	$0	$0	$0	$0	0.00%	$0	$0	$0
20	69	$0	$0	$0	$0	0.00%	$0	$0	$0
21	70	$0	$0	$0	$0	0.00%	$0	$0	$0
22	71	$0	$0	$0	$0	0.00%	$0	$0	$0
23	72	$0	$0	$0	$0	0.00%	$0	$0	$0
24	73	$0	$0	$0	$0	0.00%	$0	$0	$0
25	74	$0	$0	$0	$0	0.00%	$0	$0	$0
26	75	$0	$0	$0	$0	0.00%	$0	$0	$0
27	76	$0	$0	$0	$0	0.00%	$0	$0	$0
28	77	$0	$0	$0	$0	0.00%	$0	$0	$0
29	78	$0	$0	$0	$0	0.00%	$0	$0	$0
30	79	$0	$0	$0	$0	0.00%	$0	$0	$0
31	80	$0	$0	$0	$0	0.00%	$0	$0	$0
32	81	$0	$0	$0	$0	0.00%	$0	$0	$0
33	82	$0	$0	$0	$0	0.00%	$0	$0	$0
34	83	$0	$0	$0	$0	0.00%	$0	$0	$0
35	84	$0	$0	$0	$0	0.00%	$0	$0	$0
36	85	$0	$0	$0	$0	0.00%	$0	$0	$0
37	86	$0	$0	$0	$0	0.00%	$0	$0	$0
38	87	$0	$0	$0	$0	0.00%	$0	$0	$0
39	88	$0	$0	$0	$0	0.00%	$0	$0	$0
40	89	$0	$0	$0	$0	0.00%	$0	$0	$0
		-$14,000,000	$0	-$14,000,000			$7,661,226	$0	$7,661,226

In this case study, the goal is to insure the client with a low point death benefit of $10,000,000. In other words, in premium financing, we will typically need to start with a higher face amount because after the third-party lender payoff, the net death benefit will decrease, therefore we will design the premium financing strategy so that the *low point net death benefit* is equal to or greater than the *requested death benefit* at all times (in this case, $10,000,000). The $2,000,000 annual premiums in this 7-pay design (column 1) are 100% funded by the third-party lender (column 3). The total cumulative borrowed premium from the lender over the 10-year period is $14,000,000 (column 4). The client is then charged the *Financing Interest Rate* (column 5) on the *Cumulative Premium Financed Loan Balance* (column 4) and pays the lender the *Interest*

TO STAY INFORCE UNTIL AGE 120)

version 911169.85 FNKSTN 70.B

At This Index Credit Assumption, Death Benefit Lasts Until Age: 120

PLR: 4.90% Initial Gross Policy Face Amount: $26,156,622

9 (Cash) GAP COLLATERAL	10 HYPOTHETICAL INDEX CREDIT	11 POLICY DRAWDOWNS	12 GROSS POLICY CSV	13 POLICY CSV NET OF LOANS	14 DEATH BENEFIT NET OF LOANS	15 DEATH BENEFIT +YTY INCOME DRAWDOWN IRR	YEAR	AGE
$961,262	5.40%	$0	$1,195,305	-$804,695	$25,925,824	17904.04%	1	50
$1,320,456	5.40%	$0	$3,125,976	-$874,024	$25,792,778	1140.77%	2	51
$1,586,837	5.40%	$0	$5,159,666	-$840,334	$25,762,750	387.30%	3	52
$1,760,412	5.40%	$0	$7,302,582	-$697,418	$25,841,729	201.82%	4	53
$1,836,774	5.40%	$0	$9,560,005	-$439,995	$26,035,434	126.02%	5	54
$1,810,860	5.40%	$0	$11,937,910	-$62,090	$26,349,622	86.58%	6	55
$1,676,458	5.40%	$0	$14,443,511	$443,511	$26,791,285	63.00%	7	56
$1,220,476	5.40%	$0	$15,087,876	$1,087,876	$21,415,885	40.62%	8	57
$640,733	5.40%	$0	$15,762,925	$1,762,925	$21,415,885	30.69%	9	58
$33,206	5.40%	$0	$16,470,814	**$2,470,814**	**$21,415,885**	23.58%	10	59
$0	5.40%	-$14,000,000	$2,690,200	$2,690,200	$20,729,885	18.96%	11	60
$0	5.40%	$0	$2,926,024	$2,926,024	$20,010,271	15.55%	12	61
$0	5.40%	$0	$3,179,140	$3,179,140	$19,255,396	12.95%	13	62
$0	5.40%	$0	$3,450,210	$3,450,210	$18,463,532	10.89%	14	63
$0	5.40%	$0	$3,740,259	**$3,740,259**	**$17,632,867**	9.21%	15	64
$0	5.40%	$0	$4,050,936	$4,050,936	$16,761,499	7.80%	16	65
$0	5.40%	$0	$4,384,364	$4,384,364	$15,847,434	6.59%	17	66
$0	5.40%	$0	$4,743,102	$4,743,102	$14,888,580	5.52%	18	67
$0	5.40%	$0	$5,130,186	$5,130,186	$13,882,742	4.56%	19	68
$0	5.40%	$0	$5,549,274	**$5,549,274**	**$12,827,618**	3.67%	20	69
$0	5.40%	$0	$6,004,740	$6,004,740	$11,720,793	2.82%	21	70
$0	5.40%	$0	$6,501,944	$6,501,944	$10,578,497	2.00%	22	71
$0	5.40%	$0	$7,047,355	$7,047,355	$10,690,715	1.95%	23	72
$0	5.40%	$0	$7,641,417	$7,641,417	$10,790,801	1.89%	24	73
$0	5.40%	$0	$8,282,918	**$8,282,918**	**$10,871,161**	1.83%	25	74
$0	5.40%	-$766,123	$8,173,660	$8,173,660	$10,127,420	2.10%	26	75
$0	5.40%	-$766,123	$8,072,188	$8,072,188	$10,136,766	2.61%	27	76
$0	5.40%	-$766,123	$7,979,100	$7,979,100	$10,160,594	3.03%	28	77
$0	5.40%	-$766,123	$7,894,904	$7,894,904	$10,199,716	3.37%	29	78
$0	5.40%	-$766,123	$7,820,074	**$7,820,074**	**$10,254,922**	3.66%	30	79
$0	5.40%	-$766,123	$7,755,080	$7,755,080	$10,327,009	3.90%	31	80
$0	5.40%	-$766,123	$7,698,879	$7,698,879	$10,415,205	4.11%	32	81
$0	5.40%	-$766,123	$7,649,511	$7,649,511	$10,517,790	4.28%	33	82
$0	5.40%	-$766,123	$7,605,836	$7,605,836	$10,633,919	4.43%	34	83
$0	5.40%	-$766,123	$7,566,368	**$7,566,368**	**$10,762,403**	4.55%	35	84
$0	5.40%	$0	$8,332,709	$8,332,709	$11,705,129	4.57%	36	85
$0	5.40%	$0	$9,138,293	$9,138,293	$12,695,825	4.58%	37	86
$0	5.40%	$0	$9,982,762	$9,982,762	$13,734,448	4.59%	38	87
$0	5.40%	$0	$10,866,146	$10,866,146	$14,821,376	4.60%	39	88
$0	5.40%	$0	$11,786,702	**$11,786,702**	**$15,955,144**	4.61%	40	89

TOTAL INCOME DRAWN: -$7,661,230

Due out-of-pocket each year (column 6). In this *First-Dollar Financing (FDF)* design (one of several different financing methods I often use), there is no *Interest Accrued* (column 7), so the total *Client Contribution* each year is solely comprised of the interest payments to the lender (column 8).

I will be repeating this same ledger over the next several pages with my commentary at the bottom of each page to make it easier for you to reference the numbers in the ledger.

In premium financing, the *Gross Cash Surrender Value (GCSV)* is typically less than the outstanding loan balance in the first few years due to surrender charges and other frontloaded insurance charges. This shortfall between the *Cumulative Premium*

73

SUMMARY OF CARRIER-ILLUSTRATED STATIC RETURNS (DESIGNED)
FIRST-DOLLAR FINANCING

Health Rating: **PREFERRED** Third Party Loan Payoff Type: **PAR LOAN**

YEAR	AGE	1 TOTAL POLICY PREMIUMS	2 EQUITY PREMIUMS	3 BORROWED PREMIUMS	4 CUMULATIVE PF LOAN BALANCE	5 FINANCING INTEREST RATE	6 INTEREST DUE	7 INTEREST ACCRUED	8 CLIENT CONTRIBUTION
1	50	$2,000,000	$0	$2,000,000	$2,000,000	7.20%	$144,000	$0	$144,000
2	51	$2,000,000	$0	$2,000,000	$4,000,000	7.30%	$292,061	$0	$292,061
3	52	$2,000,000	$0	$2,000,000	$6,000,000	7.41%	$444,314	$0	$444,314
4	53	$2,000,000	$0	$2,000,000	$8,000,000	7.51%	$600,895	$0	$600,895
5	54	$2,000,000	$0	$2,000,000	$10,000,000	7.62%	$761,943	$0	$761,943
6	55	$2,000,000	$0	$2,000,000	$12,000,000	7.73%	$927,601	$0	$927,601
7	56	$2,000,000	$0	$2,000,000	$14,000,000	7.84%	$1,098,017	$0	$1,098,017
8	57	$0	$0	$0	$14,000,000	7.96%	$1,114,174	$0	$1,114,174
9	58	$0	$0	$0	$14,000,000	8.08%	$1,130,680	$0	$1,130,680
10	59	$0	$0	$0	$14,000,000	8.20%	$1,147,543	$0	$1,147,543
11	60	$0	$0	$0	$0	0.00%	$0	$0	$0
12	61	$0	$0	$0	$0	0.00%	$0	$0	$0
13	62	$0	$0	$0	$0	0.00%	$0	$0	$0
14	63	$0	$0	$0	$0	0.00%	$0	$0	$0
15	64	$0	$0	$0	$0	0.00%	$0	$0	$0
16	65	$0	$0	$0	$0	0.00%	$0	$0	$0
17	66	$0	$0	$0	$0	0.00%	$0	$0	$0
18	67	$0	$0	$0	$0	0.00%	$0	$0	$0
19	68	$0	$0	$0	$0	0.00%	$0	$0	$0
20	69	$0	$0	$0	$0	0.00%	$0	$0	$0
21	70	$0	$0	$0	$0	0.00%	$0	$0	$0
22	71	$0	$0	$0	$0	0.00%	$0	$0	$0
23	72	$0	$0	$0	$0	0.00%	$0	$0	$0
24	73	$0	$0	$0	$0	0.00%	$0	$0	$0
25	74	$0	$0	$0	$0	0.00%	$0	$0	$0
26	75	$0	$0	$0	$0	0.00%	$0	$0	$0
27	76	$0	$0	$0	$0	0.00%	$0	$0	$0
28	77	$0	$0	$0	$0	0.00%	$0	$0	$0
29	78	$0	$0	$0	$0	0.00%	$0	$0	$0
30	79	$0	$0	$0	$0	0.00%	$0	$0	$0
31	80	$0	$0	$0	$0	0.00%	$0	$0	$0
32	81	$0	$0	$0	$0	0.00%	$0	$0	$0
33	82	$0	$0	$0	$0	0.00%	$0	$0	$0
34	83	$0	$0	$0	$0	0.00%	$0	$0	$0
35	84	$0	$0	$0	$0	0.00%	$0	$0	$0
36	85	$0	$0	$0	$0	0.00%	$0	$0	$0
37	86	$0	$0	$0	$0	0.00%	$0	$0	$0
38	87	$0	$0	$0	$0	0.00%	$0	$0	$0
39	88	$0	$0	$0	$0	0.00%	$0	$0	$0
40	89	$0	$0	$0	$0	0.00%	$0	$0	$0
		-$14,000,000	$0	-$14,000,000			$7,661,226	$0	$7,661,226

Financed Loan Balance and the policy *Gross Cash Surrender Value (GCSV)* must be collateralized based on each specific lender's requirements.

In this case study, the lender gives the *Gross Cash Surrender Value (GCSV)* a 95% valuation, and a 100% valuation of the outside cash collateral posted. Using this calculation, and assuming a 5.40% policy index credit each year, the client would be required to post additional outside collateral in years 1-10 (column 9). The third-party lender is paid off in year 11 using a *Participating Loan* (column 11).

TO STAY INFORCE UNTIL AGE 120)

version 911169.85 FNKSTN 70.B

At This Index Credit Assumption, Death Benefit Lasts Until Age: 120

PLR: 4.90% Initial Gross Policy Face Amount: $26,156,622

9 (Cash) GAP COLLATERAL	10 HYPOTHETICAL INDEX CREDIT	11 POLICY DRAWDOWNS	12 GROSS POLICY CSV	13 POLICY CSV NET OF LOANS	14 DEATH BENEFIT NET OF LOANS	15 DEATH BENEFIT +YTY INCOME DRAWDOWN IRR	YEAR	AGE
$961,262	5.40%	$0	$1,195,305	-$804,695	$25,925,824	17904.04%	1	50
$1,320,456	5.40%	$0	$3,125,976	-$874,024	$25,792,778	1140.77%	2	51
$1,586,837	5.40%	$0	$5,159,666	-$840,334	$25,762,750	387.30%	3	52
$1,760,412	5.40%	$0	$7,302,582	-$697,418	$25,841,729	201.82%	4	53
$1,836,774	5.40%	$0	$9,560,005	-$439,995	$26,035,434	126.02%	5	54
$1,810,860	5.40%	$0	$11,937,910	-$62,090	$26,349,622	86.58%	6	55
$1,676,458	5.40%	$0	$14,443,511	$443,511	$26,791,285	63.00%	7	56
$1,220,476	5.40%	$0	$15,087,876	$1,087,876	$21,415,885	40.62%	8	57
$640,733	5.40%	$0	$15,762,925	$1,762,925	$21,415,885	30.69%	9	58
$33,206	5.40%	$0	$16,470,814	$2,470,814	$21,415,885	23.58%	10	59
$0	5.40%	-$14,000,000	$2,690,200	$2,690,200	$20,729,885	18.96%	11	60
$0	5.40%	$0	$2,926,024	$2,926,024	$20,010,271	15.55%	12	61
$0	5.40%	$0	$3,179,140	$3,179,140	$19,255,396	12.95%	13	62
$0	5.40%	$0	$3,450,210	$3,450,210	$18,463,532	10.89%	14	63
$0	5.40%	$0	$3,740,259	$3,740,259	$17,632,867	9.21%	15	64
$0	5.40%	$0	$4,050,936	$4,050,936	$16,761,499	7.80%	16	65
$0	5.40%	$0	$4,384,364	$4,384,364	$15,847,434	6.59%	17	66
$0	5.40%	$0	$4,743,102	$4,743,102	$14,888,580	5.52%	18	67
$0	5.40%	$0	$5,130,186	$5,130,186	$13,882,742	4.56%	19	68
$0	5.40%	$0	$5,549,274	$5,549,274	$12,827,618	3.67%	20	69
$0	5.40%	$0	$6,004,740	$6,004,740	$11,720,793	2.82%	21	70
$0	5.40%	$0	$6,501,944	$6,501,944	$10,578,497	2.00%	22	71
$0	5.40%	$0	$7,047,355	$7,047,355	$10,690,715	1.95%	23	72
$0	5.40%	$0	$7,641,417	$7,641,417	$10,790,801	1.89%	24	73
$0	5.40%	$0	$8,282,918	$8,282,918	$10,871,161	1.83%	25	74
$0	5.40%	-$766,123	$8,173,660	$8,173,660	$10,127,420	2.10%	26	75
$0	5.40%	-$766,123	$8,072,188	$8,072,188	$10,136,766	2.61%	27	76
$0	5.40%	-$766,123	$7,979,100	$7,979,100	$10,160,594	3.03%	28	77
$0	5.40%	-$766,123	$7,894,904	$7,894,904	$10,199,716	3.37%	29	78
$0	5.40%	-$766,123	$7,820,074	$7,820,074	$10,254,922	3.66%	30	79
$0	5.40%	-$766,123	$7,755,080	$7,755,080	$10,327,009	3.90%	31	80
$0	5.40%	-$766,123	$7,698,879	$7,698,879	$10,415,205	4.11%	32	81
$0	5.40%	-$766,123	$7,649,511	$7,649,511	$10,517,790	4.28%	33	82
$0	5.40%	-$766,123	$7,605,836	$7,605,836	$10,633,919	4.43%	34	83
$0	5.40%	-$766,123	$7,566,368	$7,566,368	$10,762,403	4.55%	35	84
$0	5.40%	$0	$8,332,709	$8,332,709	$11,705,129	4.57%	36	85
$0	5.40%	$0	$9,138,293	$9,138,293	$12,695,825	4.58%	37	86
$0	5.40%	$0	$9,982,762	$9,982,762	$13,734,448	4.59%	38	87
$0	5.40%	$0	$10,866,146	$10,866,146	$14,821,376	4.60%	39	88
$0	5.40%	$0	$11,786,702	$11,786,702	$15,955,144	4.61%	40	89

TOTAL INCOME DRAWN: -$7,661,230

The reason we do not see a decrease in the *Gross Accumulated Value* (column 12) is that the drawdown used to payoff the third-party lender is a *Participating Loan*, so as discussed earlier in this book, the *Gross Accumulated Value* receives the index credit each year (5.40% in this static depiction) after policy charges have been deducted.

Again, I will be repeating this same ledger over the next several pages with my commentary at the bottom of each page to make it easier for you to reference the numbers in the ledger.

SUMMARY OF CARRIER-ILLUSTRATED STATIC RETURNS (DESIGNED)
FIRST-DOLLAR FINANCING

Health Rating: **PREFERRED** Third Party Loan Payoff Type: **PAR LOAN**

YEAR	AGE	1 TOTAL POLICY PREMIUMS	2 EQUITY PREMIUMS	3 BORROWED PREMIUMS	4 CUMULATIVE PF LOAN BALANCE	5 FINANCING INTEREST RATE	6 INTEREST DUE	7 INTEREST ACCRUED	8 CLIENT CONTRIBUTION
1	50	$2,000,000	$0	$2,000,000	$2,000,000	7.20%	$144,000	$0	$144,000
2	51	$2,000,000	$0	$2,000,000	$4,000,000	7.30%	$292,061	$0	$292,061
3	52	$2,000,000	$0	$2,000,000	$6,000,000	7.41%	$444,314	$0	$444,314
4	53	$2,000,000	$0	$2,000,000	$8,000,000	7.51%	$600,895	$0	$600,895
5	54	$2,000,000	$0	$2,000,000	$10,000,000	7.62%	$761,943	$0	$761,943
6	55	$2,000,000	$0	$2,000,000	$12,000,000	7.73%	$927,601	$0	$927,601
7	56	$2,000,000	$0	$2,000,000	$14,000,000	7.84%	$1,098,017	$0	$1,098,017
8	57	$0	$0	$0	$14,000,000	7.96%	$1,114,174	$0	$1,114,174
9	58	$0	$0	$0	$14,000,000	8.08%	$1,130,680	$0	$1,130,680
10	59	$0	$0	$0	$14,000,000	8.20%	$1,147,543	$0	$1,147,543
11	60	$0	$0	$0	$0	0.00%	$0	$0	$0
12	61	$0	$0	$0	$0	0.00%	$0	$0	$0
13	62	$0	$0	$0	$0	0.00%	$0	$0	$0
14	63	$0	$0	$0	$0	0.00%	$0	$0	$0
15	64	$0	$0	$0	$0	0.00%	$0	$0	$0
16	65	$0	$0	$0	$0	0.00%	$0	$0	$0
17	66	$0	$0	$0	$0	0.00%	$0	$0	$0
18	67	$0	$0	$0	$0	0.00%	$0	$0	$0
19	68	$0	$0	$0	$0	0.00%	$0	$0	$0
20	69	$0	$0	$0	$0	0.00%	$0	$0	$0
21	70	$0	$0	$0	$0	0.00%	$0	$0	$0
22	71	$0	$0	$0	$0	0.00%	$0	$0	$0
23	72	$0	$0	$0	$0	0.00%	$0	$0	$0
24	73	$0	$0	$0	$0	0.00%	$0	$0	$0
25	74	$0	$0	$0	$0	0.00%	$0	$0	$0
26	75	$0	$0	$0	$0	0.00%	$0	$0	$0
27	76	$0	$0	$0	$0	0.00%	$0	$0	$0
28	77	$0	$0	$0	$0	0.00%	$0	$0	$0
29	78	$0	$0	$0	$0	0.00%	$0	$0	$0
30	79	$0	$0	$0	$0	0.00%	$0	$0	$0
31	80	$0	$0	$0	$0	0.00%	$0	$0	$0
32	81	$0	$0	$0	$0	0.00%	$0	$0	$0
33	82	$0	$0	$0	$0	0.00%	$0	$0	$0
34	83	$0	$0	$0	$0	0.00%	$0	$0	$0
35	84	$0	$0	$0	$0	0.00%	$0	$0	$0
36	85	$0	$0	$0	$0	0.00%	$0	$0	$0
37	86	$0	$0	$0	$0	0.00%	$0	$0	$0
38	87	$0	$0	$0	$0	0.00%	$0	$0	$0
39	88	$0	$0	$0	$0	0.00%	$0	$0	$0
40	89	$0	$0	$0	$0	0.00%	$0	$0	$0
		-$14,000,000	$0	-$14,000,000			$7,661,226	$0	$7,661,226

The *Policy Cash Surrender Value Net Of Loans* (column 13) represents the *Cash Value*, net of surrender charges, net of the third-party loan balance, and net of the internal policy participating loan balance.

The *Death Benefit Net Of Loans* hits a low point of $10,127,420 in policy year 26 (column 14), accomplishing the $10,000,000 net death benefit need.

Then between policy years 26-35 (insured ages 75-84), I designed annual drawdowns in the amount of $766,123 (column 11) totaling $7,661,230 to recover 100% of the client's interest payments they made in years 1-10.

I call this *Cost Recovery*.

TO STAY INFORCE UNTIL AGE 120)

version 911169.B5 FNKSTN 70.B

At This Index Credit Assumption, Death Benefit Lasts Until Age: 120

PLR: 4.90% Initial Gross Policy Face Amount: $26,156,622 0/...

9 (Cash) GAP COLLATERAL	10 HYPOTHETICAL INDEX CREDIT	11 POLICY DRAWDOWNS	12 GROSS POLICY CSV	13 POLICY CSV NET OF LOANS	14 DEATH BENEFIT NET OF LOANS	15 DEATH BENEFIT +YTY INCOME DRAWDOWN IRR	YEAR	AGE
$961,262	5.40%	$0	$1,195,305	-$804,695	$25,925,824	17904.04%	1	50
$1,320,456	5.40%	$0	$3,125,976	-$874,024	$25,792,778	1140.77%	2	51
$1,586,837	5.40%	$0	$5,159,666	-$840,334	$25,762,750	387.30%	3	52
$1,760,412	5.40%	$0	$7,302,582	-$697,418	$25,841,729	201.82%	4	53
$1,836,774	5.40%	$0	$9,560,005	-$439,995	$26,035,434	126.02%	5	54
$1,810,860	5.40%	$0	$11,937,910	-$62,090	$26,349,622	86.58%	6	55
$1,676,458	5.40%	$0	$14,443,511	$443,511	$26,791,285	63.00%	7	56
$1,220,476	5.40%	$0	$15,087,876	$1,087,876	$21,415,885	40.62%	8	57
$640,733	5.40%	$0	$15,762,925	$1,762,925	$21,415,885	30.69%	9	58
$33,206	5.40%	$0	$16,470,814	$2,470,814	$21,415,885	23.58%	10	59
$0	5.40%	-$14,000,000	$2,690,200	$2,690,200	$20,729,885	18.96%	11	60
$0	5.40%	$0	$2,926,024	$2,926,024	$20,010,271	15.55%	12	61
$0	5.40%	$0	$3,179,140	$3,179,140	$19,255,396	12.95%	13	62
$0	5.40%	$0	$3,450,210	$3,450,210	$18,463,532	10.89%	14	63
$0	5.40%	$0	$3,740,259	$3,740,259	$17,632,867	9.21%	15	64
$0	5.40%	$0	$4,050,936	$4,050,936	$16,761,499	7.80%	16	65
$0	5.40%	$0	$4,384,364	$4,384,364	$15,847,434	6.59%	17	66
$0	5.40%	$0	$4,743,102	$4,743,102	$14,888,580	5.52%	18	67
$0	5.40%	$0	$5,130,186	$5,130,186	$13,882,742	4.56%	19	68
$0	5.40%	$0	$5,549,274	$5,549,274	$12,827,618	3.67%	20	69
$0	5.40%	$0	$6,004,740	$6,004,740	$11,720,793	2.82%	21	70
$0	5.40%	$0	$6,501,944	$6,501,944	$10,578,497	2.00%	22	71
$0	5.40%	$0	$7,047,355	$7,047,355	$10,690,715	1.95%	23	72
$0	5.40%	$0	$7,641,417	$7,641,417	$10,790,801	1.89%	24	73
$0	5.40%	$0	$8,282,918	$8,282,918	$10,871,161	1.83%	25	74
$0	5.40%	-$766,123	$8,173,660	$8,173,660	$10,127,420	2.10%	26	75
$0	5.40%	-$766,123	$8,072,188	$8,072,188	$10,136,766	2.61%	27	76
$0	5.40%	-$766,123	$7,979,100	$7,979,100	$10,160,594	3.03%	28	77
$0	5.40%	-$766,123	$7,894,904	$7,894,904	$10,199,716	3.37%	29	78
$0	5.40%	-$766,123	$7,820,074	$7,820,074	$10,254,922	3.66%	30	79
$0	5.40%	-$766,123	$7,755,080	$7,755,080	$10,327,009	3.90%	31	80
$0	5.40%	-$766,123	$7,698,879	$7,698,879	$10,415,205	4.11%	32	81
$0	5.40%	-$766,123	$7,649,511	$7,649,511	$10,517,790	4.28%	33	82
$0	5.40%	-$766,123	$7,605,836	$7,605,836	$10,633,919	4.43%	34	83
$0	5.40%	-$766,123	$7,566,368	$7,566,368	$10,762,403	4.55%	35	84
$0	5.40%	$0	$8,332,709	$8,332,709	$11,705,129	4.57%	36	85
$0	5.40%	$0	$9,138,293	$9,138,293	$12,695,825	4.58%	37	86
$0	5.40%	$0	$9,982,762	$9,982,762	$13,734,448	4.59%	38	87
$0	5.40%	$0	$10,866,146	$10,866,146	$14,821,376	4.60%	39	88
$0	5.40%	$0	$11,786,702	$11,786,702	$15,955,144	4.61%	40	89

TOTAL INCOME DRAWN: -$7,661,230

At first glance you may be saying to yourself, *"My client is wealthy enough to the point where they wouldn't care about the cost recovery."* That is a very logical assumption, and it may even be true, however the most compelling part of a death benefit-focused design that incorporates a *Cost Recovery* feature is the emotional effect it has on the client. In this design above, I custom designed the cost recovery piece so that the total drawdowns equal the total interest the client paid in years 1-10, which creates a *zero net cost*, all the while maintaining a net death benefit that does not fall below the $10,000,000 initial request (column 14).

This method of positioning the *Cost Recovery* to create a *Zero Net Cost* is a strategic communication process of anticipating (and creating) a micro-argument wherein the client will likely argue the fact that they don't *need* the $766,123 annual drawdowns for their own retirement, and that they would rather maximize the wealth transfer outside their taxable estate by leaving the cash in the policy, pushing the increasing death benefit to its maximum.

This *argument* is sweet music to my ears because it is a sign that the client understands that <u>life insurance is not a *cost* per se, rather a more efficient *reallocation* of their liquid assets towards a more tax-efficient asset – *Premium Financed Life Insurance*</u>, that can be owned outside their taxable estate in an *Irrevocable Life Insurance Trust (ILIT)*.

The mere illustration of 100% cost recovery that creates a potential *zero net cost* is more of an *emotional* appeal, whereas leaving the money inside the policy to maximize tax-efficient wealth transfer is more of a *mathematical* appeal. However, one advisor I recently worked with *loved* the *Cost Recovery* option because he saw an opportunity for his client to use the recovered funds to invest in higher risk (and potentially higher yielding) investments, including private equity. His client previously felt such investments were too risky, however with these newfound funds, his client felt comfortable *swinging for the fences*, for these were *found* funds.

Regardless of the client's proclivity towards one design versus the other, the point is that we have shown them *optionality*, which most clients tend to appreciate. In all of my proposals, I always transparently offer the client a *non-financed* version of the same product I used in my premium financed design that satisfies their death benefit need (in this case, $10,000,000) as an alternative to my premium financed solution. I do this in an effort to transparently show them that premium financing is not the only solution available.

The following page shows a *Non-Financed IUL* using the exact same product, from the exact same carrier, using the exact same 5.40% index crediting assumption, solving for a level death benefit of $10,000,000. Both the *financed* and *non-financed* policies were designed to last until age 120, then endow.

NON-FINANCED SOLUTION

This solution requires the client to pay premiums out of pocket throughout the period shown below in the "Annual Premium" column.

NON-FINANCED IUL			5.40%
AGE	ANNUAL PREMIUM	CASH VALUE	DEATH BENEFIT
1	50	$146,356	$0	$10,000,000
2	51	$146,356	$95,264	$10,000,000
3	52	$146,356	$213,295	$10,000,000
4	53	$146,356	$335,799	$10,000,000
5	54	$146,356	$463,043	$10,000,000
6	55	$146,356	$594,873	$10,000,000
7	56	$146,356	$731,804	$10,000,000
8	57	$146,356	$874,185	$10,000,000
9	58	$146,356	$1,022,695	$10,000,000
10	59	$146,356	$1,177,625	$10,000,000
11	60	$146,356	$1,372,877	$10,000,000
12	61	$146,356	$1,577,902	$10,000,000
13	62	$146,356	$1,792,934	$10,000,000
14	63	$146,356	$2,018,030	$10,000,000
15	64	$146,356	$2,253,314	$10,000,000
16	65	$146,356	$2,499,099	$10,000,000
17	66	$146,356	$2,755,797	$10,000,000
18	67	$146,356	$3,023,878	$10,000,000
19	68	$146,356	$3,303,845	$10,000,000
20	69	$146,356	$3,596,265	$10,000,000
21	70	$0	$3,753,967	$10,000,000
22	71	$0	$3,915,561	$10,000,000
23	72	$0	$4,080,846	$10,000,000
24	73	$0	$4,249,591	$10,000,000
25	74	$0	$4,421,581	$10,000,000
26	75	$0	$4,596,621	$10,000,000
27	76	$0	$4,774,931	$10,000,000
28	77	$0	$4,956,505	$10,000,000
29	78	$0	$5,141,250	$10,000,000
30	79	$0	$5,329,191	$10,000,000
31	80	$0	$5,520,559	$10,000,000
32	81	$0	$5,713,073	$10,000,000
33	82	$0	$5,903,825	$10,000,000
34	83	$0	$6,092,241	$10,000,000
35	84	$0	$6,277,912	$10,000,000
36	85	$0	$6,460,358	$10,000,000
37	86	$0	$6,639,576	$10,000,000
38	87	$0	$6,816,220	$10,000,000
39	88	$0	$6,991,809	$10,000,000
40	89	$0	$7,166,807	$10,000,000

$2,927,120 TOTAL NET COST (OVER 40 YEARS)

PREMIUM FINANCED w/ COST RECOVERY

In this solution, the client is borrowing all of the premiums from a third party lender paying interest out-of-pocket.

FIRST-DOLLAR FINANCING			5.40%
AGE	ANNUAL CONTRIBUTION	CASH VALUE NET OF LOANS	DEATH BENEFIT NET OF LOANS
1	50	$144,000	$0	$25,925,824
2	51	$292,061	$0	$25,792,778
3	52	$444,314	$0	$25,762,750
4	53	$600,895	$0	$25,841,729
5	54	$761,943	$0	$26,035,434
6	55	$927,601	$0	$26,349,622
7	56	$1,098,017	$443,511	$26,791,285
8	57	$1,114,174	$1,087,876	$21,415,885
9	58	$1,130,680	$1,762,925	$21,415,885
10	59	$1,147,543	$2,470,814	$21,415,885
11	60	$0	$2,690,200	$20,729,885
12	61	$0	$2,926,024	$20,010,271
13	62	$0	$3,179,140	$19,255,396
14	63	$0	$3,450,210	$18,463,532
15	64	$0	$3,740,259	$17,632,867
16	65	$0	$4,050,936	$16,761,499
17	66	$0	$4,384,364	$15,847,434
18	67	$0	$4,743,102	$14,888,580
19	68	$0	$5,130,186	$13,882,742
20	69	$0	$5,549,274	$12,827,618
21	70	$0	$6,004,740	$11,720,793
22	71	$0	$6,501,944	$10,578,497
23	72	$0	$7,047,355	$10,690,715
24	73	$0	$7,641,417	$10,790,801
25	74	$0	$8,282,918	$10,871,161
26	75	-$766,123	$8,173,660	$10,127,420
27	76	-$766,123	$8,072,188	$10,136,766
28	77	-$766,123	$7,979,100	$10,160,594
29	78	-$766,123	$7,894,904	$10,199,716
30	79	-$766,123	$7,820,074	$10,254,922
31	80	-$766,123	$7,755,080	$10,327,009
32	81	-$766,123	$7,698,879	$10,415,205
33	82	-$766,123	$7,649,511	$10,517,790
34	83	-$766,123	$7,605,836	$10,633,919
35	84	-$766,123	$7,566,368	$10,762,403
36	85	$0	$8,332,709	$11,705,129
37	86	$0	$9,138,293	$12,695,825
38	87	$0	$9,982,762	$13,734,448
39	88	$0	$10,866,146	$14,821,376
40	89	$0	$11,786,702	$15,955,144

$0 TOTAL NET COST AFTER $7.66MM COST RECOVERY DRAWDOWNS

The premium on the *Non-Financed Policy* is $146,356 per year for twenty years, equaling $2,927,120 in total client outlay (see the table above on the left), versus approximately $7,661,230 in cumulative interest payments in the *First-Dollar Financing (FDF)* design above… however that $7,661,230 cost is recovered through tax-free *Participating Loans* in years 26-35, creating a *zero net cost* (see the table above on the right). In addition, the net death benefit

79

in the *First-Dollar Financing (FDF)* design increases far beyond the $10,000,000 requested amount from age 85 and on. The following bar graph which shows the difference in net death benefit outcomes between the non-financed option and the financed option. It also shows a *Non-Insurance Based Alternative Asset* growing at the same 5.40% gross return, taxable at both capital gains and estate tax rates noted in the legend at the bottom of the graph below.

	5.40% ALTERNATIVE ASSET
1	$88,758
2	$271,201
3	$552,470
4	$937,929
5	$1,433,176
6	$2,044,051
7	$2,776,641
8	$3,539,187
9	$4,332,723
10	$5,158,313
11	$5,299,120
12	$5,443,770
13	$5,592,368
14	$5,745,023
15	$5,901,845
16	$6,062,948
17	$6,228,448
18	$6,398,466
19	$6,573,125
20	$6,752,551
21	$6,936,876
22	$7,126,232
23	$7,320,757
24	$7,520,591
25	$7,725,881
26	$7,464,553
27	$7,196,091
28	$6,920,301
29	$6,636,983
30	$6,345,931
31	$6,046,935
32	$5,739,776
33	$5,424,234
34	$5,100,077
35	$4,767,073
36	$4,897,199
37	$5,030,878
38	$5,168,206
39	$5,309,283
40	$5,454,210

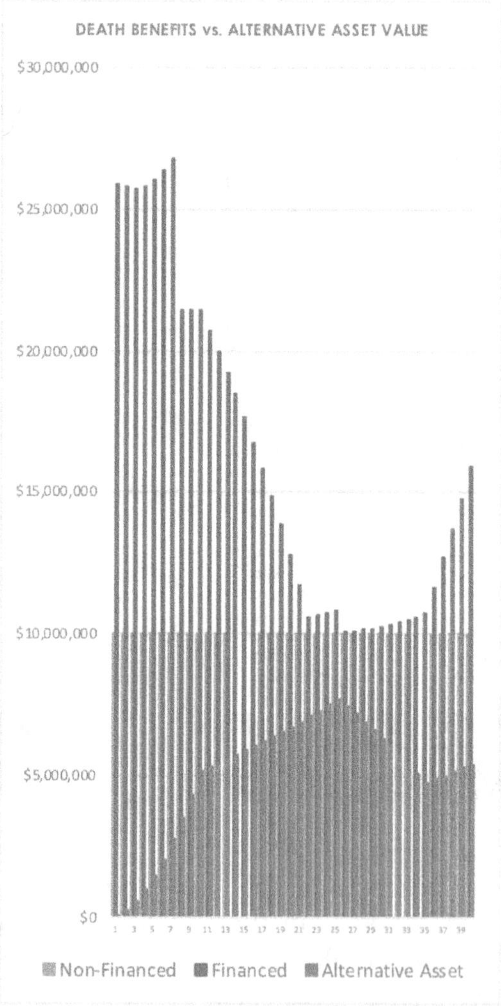

DEATH BENEFITS vs. ALTERNATIVE ASSET VALUE

■ Non-Financed ■ Financed ■ Alternative Asset

Taxable Gains Rate Assumption: 32.60%
Estate Tax Rate Assumption: 40.00%
Investment Fee Assumption: 1.35%

The light grey bars illustrate the ongoing *Death Benefit Net Of Loans* in the *Financed* policy over the course of forty years. As you see, the face amount is substantially higher than the requested amount in the beginning, and drops down to a lowpoint of just above $10,000,000, and even with a 100% *Cost Recovery* via policy drawdowns (creating a *zero net cost*), the *Death Benefit Net Of Loans* remains north of the low point for the entire period.

The medium grey bars illustrate the ongoing level $10,000,000 *Death Benefit* in the *Non-Financed* policy. Again, there is no *Cost Recovery* in this scenario, hence the total cost of twenty years of $146,356 annual premiums is $2,927,120 (versus a *zero net cost* in the *Financed* policy).

The dark grey bars represent a *Non-Insurance Based Alternative Asset* growing at the same gross return as both the *Financed* and *Non-Financed* policies' index credit (in this case, 5.40%). The ongoing net amount transferred to *Generation Two* of this asset assumes a 32.60% *Capital Gains Tax Rate*, a 1.35% all-in investment fee, and a 40.00% *Estate Tax Rate*.

I think it is always important to explain the alternative options to clients, transparently showing them comparisons other than *Premium Financed Life Insurance*.

In most cases (depending on the client's age, health, and financial situation), the *Premium Financed Life Insurance* solution provides a superior potential outcome from the standpoint of:

1. Risk Mitigation.
2. Certainty.
3. Leverage.
4. Taxation.
5. Liquidity.
6. Generational Wealth Preservation.
7. Inter-Family Relationship Preservation.

Despite the obvious benefits, the biggest objection to this proposition usually revolves around cost. Even financing large life insurance policies requires a substantial client outlay (assuming they aren't falling for the illusion of *free insurance*). I have an entire chapter in this book dedicated to dispelling the myths of so-called *free insurance* wherein the client merely posts collateral and pays no interest payments.

My *Zero Net Cost* platform has the client pay the proper out-of-pocket expense, then recover that cost via policy drawdowns. But let's take away the *Cost Recovery* element for just a moment.

The reality is that the client's payments into a *Premium Financed Life Insurance* arrangement isn't actually a *cost* per se. It is a mere reallocation of assets, switching out a *non-tax efficient* asset (a taxable asset like stocks, bonds, real estate, etc.) for a *more tax-efficient* asset (the life insurance policy in an ILIT).

To illustrate the concept of *"reallocating assets is not a cost,"* the chart on the next page shows a $10,000,000 investment portfolio inside the client's taxable estate growing at the same 5.40% as the policy index credit.

It also assumes 32.60% in capital gains tax, 1.35% as an all-in investment fee, and 40.00% in estate taxes.

Column 1 shows the net value of this account that *Generation Two (G2)* would inherit if death of the second spouse were to occur in any given year.

Column 2 shows the exact same investment portfolio, less the interest payments due on the premium financing loan (column 3), as well as the *Participating Loan Cost Recovery* drawdowns in years 26-35 which get invested back into the *Non-Insurance Based Alternative Asset*.

Column 4 shows this same amount, plus the life insurance policy death benefit (net of loans).

PREMIUM FINANCED LIFE INSURANCE

Year	Age	1 CURRENT PORTFOLIO NET VALUE AT DEATH (NO LIFE INSURANCE)		2 CURRENT PORTFOLIO THAT REPOSITIONS SOME CAPITAL INTO LIFE		3 AMOUNT REPOSITIONED INTO LIFE INSURANCE		4 TOTAL PORTFOLIO NET VALUE AT DEATH (WITH LIFE INSURANCE)
1	50	$6,163,782	vs	$6,075,024	-	$144,000	=	$32,000,848
2	51	$6,332,035	vs	$6,060,834	-	$292,061	=	$31,853,612
3	52	$6,504,880	vs	$5,952,411	-	$444,314	=	$31,715,161
4	53	$6,682,444	vs	$5,744,515	-	$600,895	=	$31,586,244
5	54	$6,864,855	vs	$5,431,678	-	$761,943	=	$31,467,112
6	55	$7,052,245	vs	$5,008,194	-	$927,601	=	$31,357,816
7	56	$7,244,750	vs	$4,468,109	-	$1,098,017	=	$31,259,394
8	57	$7,442,510	vs	$3,903,323	-	$1,114,174	=	$25,319,208
9	58	$7,645,668	vs	$3,312,945	-	$1,130,680	=	$24,728,830
10	59	$7,854,372	vs	$2,696,059	-	$1,147,543	=	$24,111,944
11	60	$8,068,772	vs	$2,769,653	-	$0	=	$23,499,538
12	61	$8,289,026	vs	$2,845,256	-	$0	=	$22,855,527
13	62	$8,515,291	vs	$2,922,923	-	$0	=	$22,178,319
14	63	$8,747,733	vs	$3,002,710	-	$0	=	$21,466,242
15	64	$8,986,520	vs	$3,084,675	-	$0	=	$20,717,542
16	65	$9,231,825	vs	$3,168,877	-	$0	=	$19,930,376
17	66	$9,483,826	vs	$3,255,378	-	$0	=	$19,102,812
18	67	$9,742,706	vs	$3,344,240	-	$0	=	$18,232,820
19	68	$10,008,653	vs	$3,435,528	-	$0	=	$17,318,270
20	69	$10,281,859	vs	$3,529,308	-	$0	=	$16,356,926
21	70	$10,562,523	vs	$3,625,647	-	$0	=	$15,346,440
22	71	$10,850,848	vs	$3,724,616	-	$0	=	$14,303,113
23	72	$11,147,044	vs	$3,826,287	-	$0	=	$14,517,002
24	73	$11,451,325	vs	$3,930,733	-	$0	=	$14,721,534
25	74	$11,763,911	vs	$4,038,031	-	$0	=	$14,909,192
26	75	$12,085,031	vs	$4,620,478	-	-$766,123	=	$14,747,898
27	76	$12,414,916	vs	$5,218,825	-	-$766,123	=	$15,355,591
28	77	$12,753,806	vs	$5,833,505	-	-$766,123	=	$15,994,099
29	78	$13,101,947	vs	$6,464,963	-	-$766,123	=	$16,664,679
30	79	$13,459,590	vs	$7,113,659	-	-$766,123	=	$17,368,581
31	80	$13,826,997	vs	$7,780,062	-	-$766,123	=	$18,107,071
32	81	$14,204,432	vs	$8,464,656	-	-$766,123	=	$18,879,861
33	82	$14,592,171	vs	$9,167,937	-	-$766,123	=	$19,685,727
34	83	$14,990,493	vs	$9,890,416	-	-$766,123	=	$20,524,335
35	84	$15,399,689	vs	$10,632,616	-	-$766,123	=	$21,395,019
36	85	$15,820,054	vs	$10,922,855	-	$0	=	$22,627,984
37	86	$16,251,894	vs	$11,221,016	-	$0	=	$23,916,841
38	87	$16,695,522	vs	$11,527,316	-	$0	=	$25,261,764
39	88	$17,151,260	vs	$11,841,977	-	$0	=	$26,663,353
40	89	$17,619,438	vs	$12,165,228	-	$0	=	$28,120,372

Column 1 = After-Tax Value Of The Portfolio Without Life Insurance
Column 4 = After-Tax Value Of The Portfolio With Life Insurance

The graph below that shows the same scenario using the same assumptions of growth, fees, and taxes in the *Non-Insurance Based Investment Portfolio*, with and without incorporating premium financed life insurance in the overall estate plan.

As you can see, the light grey line in the graph (the combination of the *Non-Insurance Based Investment Portfolio* with the *Premium Financed Life Insurance* death benefit) severely outperforms the dark grey line which represents exact same portfolio construction where no drawdowns are taken to fund a *Premium Financed Life Insurance* policy.

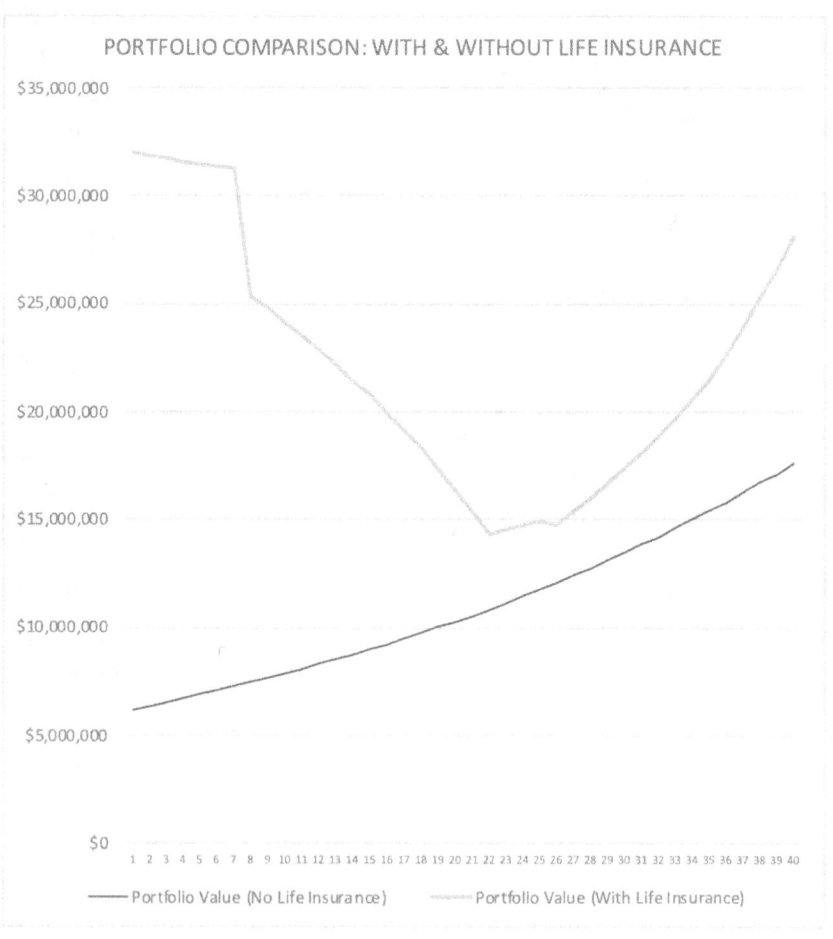

Thus far, I have only reviewed one of my premium financing platforms, however I have several others. Some are what I call hybrid premium financing loan models wherein the client pays some of the premiums out-of-pocket and finances the remaining premiums. Sometimes, the client will pay the interest due on the loan balance each year, and sometimes they will accrue the interest.

If they are accruing interest, these models still require the client to have some *skin in the game*. These are not *free insurance* programs whatsoever.

Each of these loan models is designed to suit a very specific type of client, based on their age, health rating, net worth, liquidity, risk tolerance, and of course, their specific needs throughout the chronological stages of their life.

In the following chapters, I will model several of my alternative premium financing platforms and I will discuss when each one is most suitable for a specific type of client.

These additional models are:

1. Second-Year Financing (2YF)
2. Partial-Equity Interest Accrual (PEIA)
3. Third-Year Financing (3YF)
4. Sixth-Year Financing (6YF)

DARREN SUGIYAMA

Chapter 11
Second-Year Financing (2YF)

In this alternative premium financing design, the concept is to post the collateral *inside* the policy by paying the first-year premium out-of-pocket (non-financed) , then begin financing premiums in policy year two, hence the term *Second-Year Financing (2YF)*. There are several advantages of constructing *Premium Financed Life Insurance* using this loan structure which I will discuss in this chapter.

I used this method of financing with my wife's policy. She owned a non-financed *Whole Life* policy, and we decided to 1035 its cash value into an *IUL*, which served as the first-year premium in the new policy, and we began financing the remaining premiums starting in year two. In this design we decided to pay the interest on the borrowed premiums out-of-pocket each year thereafter.

I also used the *Second-Year Financing (2YF)* loan design on my own policy as well. I didn't 1035 any pre-existing policy value, rather I paid the first-year premium out-of-pocket, and started financing premiums in the second year. I used one of my S-corp entities as the owner of the policy, beneficiary of the death benefit, and borrower of the premium financing loan. My S-corp pays the interest due each year.

Back then, when I explained this method of *delayed* financing to several people in the industry, they criticized me, saying that I wasn't taking full advantage of maximizing leverage by borrowing 100% of the premiums. They obviously didn't understand the merits of this methodology. Now, I'm not saying that this method is *always* better than *First-Dollar Financing (FDF)* for every single client out there, but it *is* ideal for a particular type of client (like I was at that time). I had the liquidity to pay the first-year premium, and in this chapter, I will explain why I (and certain types of clients) prefer this method over *First-Dollar Financing (FDF)*.

As an example, there are some clients that prefer to pay a larger down payment when purchasing real estate, and mortgaging less of the purchase, creating a stronger *Loan-To-Value (LTV)* ratio by incurring less debt. This also reduces their mortgage payments because they are borrowing less.

This concept can be applied to *Premium Financed Life Insurance* as well, slightly deleveraging the proposition.

The biggest element I like about *Second-Year Financing (2YF)* – and the reason why I chose this method of financing my own policy – is that the policy cash value will most likely serve as the sole collateral, with no foreseeable collateral calls.

I have found that no matter how optimistic a client is regarding their ability (and willingness) to post more collateral in the future, when the time comes, it always gives them heartburn.

Often times clients will *conveniently* come down with a case of *collateral amnesia*, and they will typically take out their emotional frustration on the advisor. The same client that said they could handle risk and volatility can easily turn into an accusatory *finger-pointer*, claiming the advisor promised they would never have to post more than the collateral amounts depicted in the original proposal.

Or even worse, if the client posted marketable securities as collateral, and their portfolio value decreases due to market conditions, the lender will require them to *true-up* the collateral shortfall.

As an example, this past year I had a *First-Dollar Financing (FDF)* client that posted one of their investment portfolios as collateral. His portfolio took heavy positions in *Amazon* and *Tesla* stock, and it just so happened that during his particular twelve-month segment (his annual point-to-point loan term period), these two stocks took tremendous hits, decreasing his overall portfolio value by 30%. As a result, the lender required him to post more collateral to make up the 30% shortfall.

Fortunately, I do a suitability study up front to make sure my clients can absorb these types of market turns, and this particular

PREMIUM FINANCED LIFE INSURANCE

client had plenty of liquid to cover the shortfall. He ended up posting additional liquid assets, and it was not a big deal.

However, imagine if a client thought they would have enough to cover a shortfall, but due to market conditions, the value of their liquid assets plummeted to the point where they couldn't cover the collateral shortfall. In my opinion, there are far too many premium financing arrangements executed by my competitors that should have never been transacted in the first place. The assumptions that were made in the original design may have worked on paper during rosy times, but add in some market volatility, combined with a borrowing interest rate hike, and all of a sudden, the client can find themselves in a compromised position.

Conversely, my own policy was structured so that the collateral was posted *inside* the policy in the form of *premium / cash value*. It just so happened that my twelve-month segment was almost identical to the client I just mentioned, so in theory, I would have been in a similar predicament. However I was not, because when the market tanked 30% at the end of my annual segment, my cash value didn't tank 30% due to the 0% floor. Sure, my *Cash Surrender Value* decreased slightly due to the policy charges that year, but it didn't take a 30% hit the way the aforementioned client's collateral did.

I have never had to post outside collateral on my own premium financing loan, nor on my wife's loan. This is a huge advantage for the type of client that either can't afford to take the risk of not being able to cover a collateral shortfall, or just doesn't have the risk tolerance profile to be able to endure such uncertainty. At the time I put my policy (and my wife's policy) in force, I was not in a place where I felt comfortable getting a collateral call if the market took a beating, however I had enough liquid to cover the first-year premium. For me, this was a great choice given where I was at that time, financially.

In addition, when it comes time to payoff the third-party lender, I won't need to drawdown 100% of my policy premiums because I didn't borrow the first-year premium. This also strengthens the long-term *Net Cash Value*. Since *Cash Value* is what sustains the policy over time (when short-paying the premiums), in order to arrive at the same *low point* death benefit as a *First-Dollar Financing (FDF)* design, the annual premium is approximately 25% less.

As an example, to arrive at the same $10,000,000 in low point death benefit on a 50-year old male with a preferred health rating, in a *First-Dollar Financing (FDF)* design, it would require $2,000,000 in annual premium borrowed on a 7-pay, with a third-party loan payoff in year 11.

However in a *Second-Year Financing (2YF)* design on the same client, it would only require $1,500,000 in annual premium on a 7-pay (only six years of which are borrowed), with a third-party loan payoff in year 11.

In this particular case study, the *Second-Year Financing (2YF)* design saves the client $1,567,933 in cumulative interest expense ($7,661,226 - $6,093,293 = $1,567,933) in comparison to the more traditional *First-Dollar Financing (FDF)* design.

	FIRST-DOLLAR FINANCING FDF	SECOND-YEAR FINANCING 2YF
Peak Collateral:	$1,836,774	$0
Annual Premium Borrowed:	$2,000,000 x 7 Years	$1,500,000 x 6 years
Total Premium Borrowed ($):	$14,000,000	$9,000,000
Total Interest Expense:	**$7,661,226**	**$6,093,293**

As I said earlier, the *Second-Year Financing (2YF)* design is not unilaterally *better* than the *First-Dollar Financing (FDF)* design, but for the right client, it can be more appropriate given their liquidity, risk tolerance, and general feelings about the concept of slightly deleveraging their premium financing arrangement.

Chapter 12
Partial-Equity Interest Accrual (PEIA)

Despite my disdain for over-leveraged *Free* or *Semi-Free Premium Financed Life Insurance* schemes, there are mathematically prudent premium financing strategies that employ *interest accrual*, but require the client to pay some out-of-pocket premiums, then borrow the remaining premiums from a third-party lender, and accrue the interest due.

<u>If they are putting enough *skin-in-the-game*, accruing interest is not necessarily a bad thing to do.</u>

One method I developed is called *Partial-Equity Interest Accrual (PEIA)* wherein the client pays approximately 33% of the premium (sometimes more, sometimes less), borrows 67% of the premiums, then accrues 100% of the interest due.

This is typically done when the client wants to contribute a set annual budget instead of varying interest payments each year.

Back in 2021 when I published the *First Edition* of this book, interest rates were substantially lower than they are today. With some clients (assuming they were extremely liquid), borrowing rates were low enough for the client to only pay 10% of the premium, borrow 90%, and accrue the interest.

When borrowing rates are sub-2%, compounding debt on 90% borrowed premiums is not problematic. However when borrowing rates are north of 7%, it is a different story, hence in today's environment, I suggest contributing a minimum of 33% of the premium if you're going to accrue interest on the borrowed premium (in this case, 67% of the premium would be borrowed).

Some intermediary firms are cheating the system when showing clients that they can pay as little as 10% of premiums (and sometimes even less), borrow 90% (and sometimes even more), and accrue interest. They make their magic trick on their spreadsheet work by showing much lower borrowing rates than exist today. Could interest rates drop as much as they are showing in their

91

illustrations? It is possible, but I don't think any client should make financial decisions based on the expectation that interest rates are going to fall that dramatically, because if they don't the client will be put in a compromised position.

It is just as egregiously irresponsible to tell a client they can just pay interest payments in the first few years, then accrue the rest. Sadly, I still see these ridiculous designs today.

Below is an infographic that outlines how the *PEIA* platform works, but just remember, in today's environment, the client should be paying at least 33% of the premium if they are going to accrue the interest on the remaining borrowed premiums.

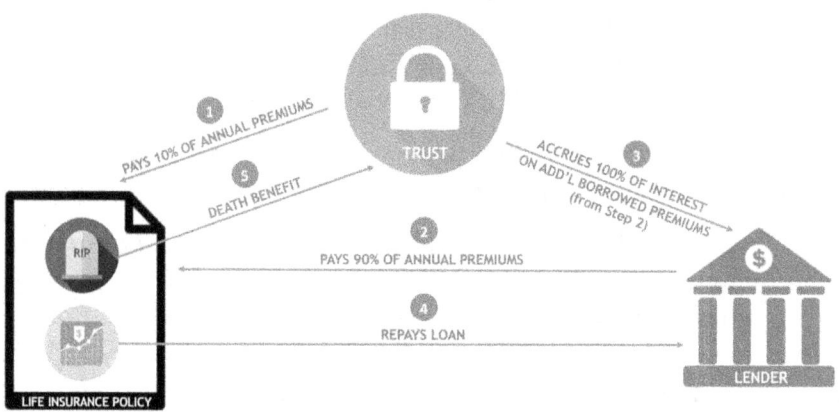

It should also be noted that in many cases, our *Partial-Equity Interest Accrual (PEIA)* platform could also be combined with our *100% Cost Recovery* strategy as well.

The idea of recovering 100% of the out-of-pocket expense has been extremely intriguing to virtually every client I have ever talked to. This is somewhat ironic because if the policy is being used for estate planning purposes, recovering this cost just pulls the value back into the client's taxable estate, making it subject to estate taxes when it transfers to the next generation. It would be more mathematically prudent to leave that cash in the policy owned by an *ILIT* outside the taxable estate, and maximize the tax-free death benefit.

In reality, it would only make sense to take drawdowns from the policy value if the client wanted to:

1. Use those funds to invest in a higher risk investment class that could potentially yield higher returns, or…

2. Use those funds to pay trust expenses, or…

3. Emotionally feel like they "got their money back."

You would be amazed at how appealing reason #3 has been to many of the clients I have personally talked to.

Even though most of them admit that they will probably leave the cash in the policy (because they don't anticipate needing it to live on), they love the idea of not incurring a net expense to fund their life insurance policy due to the *100% Cost Recovery*.

Regardless of how wealthy a person is, the emotional gratification of "getting all of their money back" is incredibly appealing, and regardless of how mathematically driven I am, I do understand the importance of optics and the client's emotions.

Using the *Partial-Equity Interest Accrual (PEIA)* model can be very attractive for a client that wants to pay a flat dollar amount each year, not having to think about the variable expense of interest each year.

As an apples-to-apples comparison, using the same male 50-year old with a preferred health rating, if the goal was to net a low point death benefit of $10,000,000, with the same 100% cost recovery strategy we discussed in the *First-Dollar Financing (FDF)* model, it would require the same $2,000,000 in annual premium, but on a 10-pay instead of a 7-pay.

The client would pay $675,000 per year (33.75% of the $2,000,000 premium), borrow the remaining $1,325,000 (66.25% of the remaining premium), and accrue the interest. The loan exit would still be in year 11 using a participating loan.

	FIRST-DOLLAR FINANCING	PARTIAL-EQUITY INTEREST ACCRUAL
	FDF	**PEIA**
Peak Collateral:	$1,836,774	$286,282
Annual Premium Borrowed:	$2,000,000 x 7 Years	$1,325,000 x 10 years
Total Premium Borrowed ($):	$14,000,000	$13,250,000
Total Outlay:	**$7,661,226**	**$6,750,000**

In the *FDF, 2YF,* and *PEIA* models, the client has *skin in the game,* which is important in any premium financing model. In the *free insurance* models, the lack of *skin-in-the-game* is what falsely leads a client to believe in the absence of risk variables.

As an example, on March 26, 2022, *Forbes* published an article about a large premium financed lawsuit wherein a client sued the advisor, the intermediary, and the carriers, claiming they all misrepresented the premium financing proposition.

Later that year on September 22, 2022, *The Wall Street Journal* reported on this lawsuit as well. In short, the client was an entertainment-industry executive who premium financed $40 million of *free* life insurance. The Forbes article says, *"It wasn't long before his free life insurance policy wasn't free."*

The client received larger-than-expected collateral calls, and the majority of their net worth was held in illiquid assets including real estate and retirement accounts. The client ended up surrendering their policies and claimed seven figures in damages in the lawsuit. If you would like to learn more about these articles, I did a webinar wherein I picked apart both of these articles, commenting on both the merits and fallacies of the journalists' perspectives. I posted a recording of this webinar video on my firm's website at: *https://www.lionsmarkcapital.com/wsj-forbes-lawsuit-commentary*

As an advisor, there is no reason to put your client (or yourself) in such a risky predicament. The only reason advisors have promoted this concept is that they think it's an easy sale and an easy commission (which are arguably the worst reasons to promote anything).

In my humble opinion, this is an irresponsible, greedy, and manipulative proposition sold by unscrupulous (and/or unintelligent) advisors who do not have the ability to properly articulate the true merits of responsible leverage and the fundamentals of properly structured *Premium Financed Life Insurance*.

Not having any *skin-in-the-game* is an attempt to get *something-for-nothing*, and if that doesn't activate your *bullshit radar*, then perhaps you should buy the rest of the Brooklyn Bridge from George C. Parker, and a few cases of snake oil from Clark Stanley.

But as much as I like the *Partial-Equity Interest Accrual (PEIA)* model – due to its simplicity regarding the client experience – I like my new *Third-Year Financing (3YF)* model even better, which I will discuss in the next chapter.

Chapter 13
Third-Year Financing (3YF)

I started designing this loan architecture several years ago, and it has evolved greatly since then. A big part of this design evolution was inspired by the increasing interest rate environment.

Though it began as a way to fix the annual client contributions (similar to the spirit of *PEIA*), and though it was originally designed to generate tax-free retirement income, <u>I have found it to be perhaps the most efficient way to design a death benefit focused case, ever</u>.

It will likely require zero outside collateral, and if outside collateral is required towards the end of the 10-year window, it will likely be de minimis. In fact, I actually prefer to show the client a requirement to post this small amount of collateral in the proposal because it plants the seed that it is *possible* that they may have to post a bit of outside collateral. I would rather set this expectation up front, and then deliver the good news that it is unnecessary when the time comes... versus lead them to expect a zero outside collateral situation, only to deliver the bad news later, even as de minimis that amount may be.

As an advisor, much of the success you will have in *Premium Financed Life Insurance* is based on the client expectations you set from the very beginning. This takes communication skill, proper positioning technique, and true confidence (which most advisors don't have). Above all, your intentions must be rooted in mathematical truth and transparency for the benefit of the client.

As an extreme example, when I started dating my wife, I had recently built a very successful business, and on our first date, I asked her how she felt about prenuptial agreements. Most men don't have the guts to have this conversation up front, so they date for months (or even years), and after they buy the ring, propose, and make wedding plans, they hesitantly bring up the subject.

Often times this blows up the entire relationship.

If you know you're going to have the conversation at some point, it is best to have it transparently up front at the beginning of the relationship. It is a more honorable and *fair* thing to do.

Yes, I'm serious when I say I brought up the topic of prenuptial agreements on our first date. My wife's response was epic.

She told me, *"I don't know why any woman would want to name claim to something she wasn't part of building. I can build my own empire."*

I practically fell in love with her on the spot.

She already had her own successful career and didn't *need* my money. Before we got married, we both signed the prenup, but once we got married, I said, *"Okay, let's combine all our bank accounts. I'm all in."*

You see, I just wanted to verify her intentions up front. The fact that she signed the prenup let me know what her expectations and intentions were. This was my version of under-promising, then over-delivering.

If you disagree with prenuptial agreements, please don't let my analogy derail you from my point. My point is, it is always best (and most honorable) to be truthful and transparent up front, even if the truth might result in a challenging conversation. A challenging conversation – if both parties are honest and transparent – will typically either strengthen the relationship and trust, or it will end a relationship that never should have started in the first place.

I take the same approach with *Premium Financed Life Insurance* clients. Full transparency and authenticity are two hallmarks of how I run my business, as well as how I live my personal life under the samurai principles known as *The Bushidō Code*. If you're interested in learning more about these principles, I recommend reading another one of my books – *The Takeo Effect*.

In the *Third-Year Financing (3YF)* model, the premium schedule and design is a bit *funky*. I design the policy using a

PREMIUM FINANCED LIFE INSURANCE

minimum face amount solve, with a max-funded premium, however the premium schedule is custom designed.

Comparing this model to the previously aforementioned designs (*FDF, 2YF,* and *PEIA*), we will use the same 50-year old male with a preferred health rating. For the purpose of consistency, we will use the same $675,000 annual budget we used in the *PEIA* model. We will also aim for a $10,000,000 low point net death benefit.

In years 1-2, the actual policy premium will be $675,000, non-financed.

In years 3-10, the actual policy premium is approximately four times larger than the premiums in years 1-2.

Each case is different based on the age and health of the client, however I am over-simplifying it for the purpose of explaining this methodology to you.

In years 3-10, the policy premiums are $2,700,000 ($675,000 x 4). During this period, the client would continue to pay the flat $675,000 annually, borrow $2,025,000, and accrue the interest.

It is important to note that the premium in years 1-2 are not *underfunded* premiums. These premiums are max-funded premiums based on a minimum death benefit solve.

3YF: THIRD-YEAR FINANCING

YEAR	AGE	TOTAL POLICY PREMIUMS	EQUITY PREMIUMS	YEARS 1-2 PREMIUM PAID BY CLIENT (100%)	LATIVE PF BALANCE	FINANCING INTEREST RATE	INTEREST DUE	(Cash) GAP COLLATERAL	POLICY DRAWDOWNS
1	50	$675,000	$675,000	$0	$0	7.20%	$0	$0	$0
2	51	$675,000	$675,000	$0	$0	7.30%	$0	$0	$0
3	52	$2,700,000	$675,000	$2,025,000	$2,025,000	7.41%	$149,956	$0	$0
4	53	$2,700,000	$675,000	$2,025,000	$4,199,956	7.51%	$315,466	$0	$0
5	54	$2,700,000	$675,000	$2,025,000	$6,540,422	7.62%	$498,343	$0	$0
6	55	$2,700,000	$675,000	$2,025,000	$9,063,765	7.73%	$700,630	$0	$0
7	56	$2,700,000	$675,000	$2,025,000	$11,789,395	7.84%	$924,639	$0	$0
8	57	$2,700,000	$675,000	$2,025,000	$14,739,034	7.96%	$1,172,989	$0	$0
9	58	$2,700,000	$675,000	$2,025,000	$17,937,023	8.08%	$1,448,645	$0	$0
10	59	$2,700,000	$675,000	$2,025,000	$21,410,668	8.20%	$1,754,975	$187,186	$0
11	60	$0	$0	$0	$0	0.00%	$0	$0	

- **25%** OF PREMIUM PAID IN YEARS 3-10
- **75%** OF PREMIUM BORROWED IN YEARS 3-10
- **100%** OF INTEREST DUE IS ACCRUED
- **DRASTICALLY REDUCED COLLATERAL**
- **PAYOFF PF LOAN**

* 100% COST RECOVERY
* LOW POINT DEATH BENEFIT >$10MM

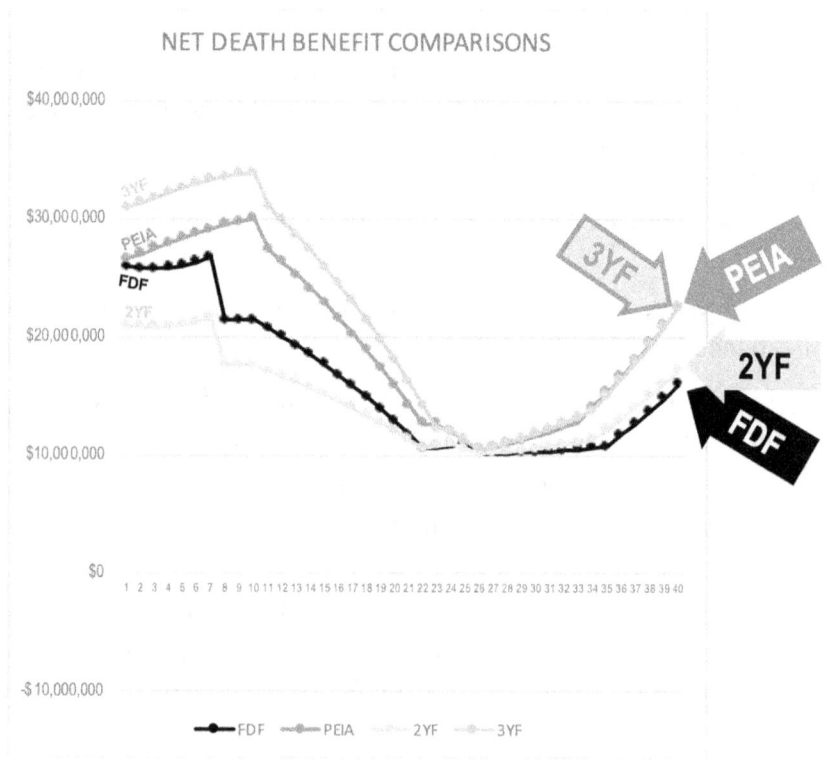

In each one of these designs (considering the comparison chart above), 100% of the client contributions are recovered using policy loans, all the while maintaining a low point death benefit above the required $10,000,000 watermark. See the ongoing net death benefit amounts of the four different premium financing designs.

The *Third-Year Financing (3YF)* design starts with a higher initial net face amount than the other three designs, and though all four designs have a similar low point net death benefit, the *Third-Year Financing (3YF)* design nets a higher net death benefit before and after the low point than the other three designs.

In addition, due to the current high interest rate environment, the *Third-Year Financing (3YF)* design doesn't incorporate third-party lending until the third year. This makes the current high interest rate environment irrelevant. It seems illogical that interest rates wouldn't fall over the next two years, however in our modeling, we still show an artificially increasing borrowing rate. As you saw in the loan model on the previous page, we showed a starting borrowing rate of 7.20% (which doesn't affect the model since there is no borrowing happening initially), however we also show the borrowing interest rate increasing to 8.20% by the tenth year (100bps higher).

This conservative depiction I model is extremely pessimistic because based on the *Forward Yield Curve Rates* at the time I modeled these cases, the expected interest rate in year 10 would only be 5.78%, versus the 8.20% rate we are illustrating.

Again, our models and stress-testing methodologies seek to under-promise and over-deliver.

One of the most important things you must understand about *Premium Financed Life Insurance* is that there are many different disciplines and designs within this category.

Premium Financed Life Insurance is a general category, similar to certain ethnic foods as a *category*.

For example, *Asian food* is a general *category* of ethnic food, but within this general category, there are several sub-categories including but not limited to Japanese food, Chinese food, Korean food, Vietnamese food, Indian food, etc.

Yes, these types of ethnic foods would fall into the category of *Asian food*, however they are all quite different. Sure some of them share similar ingredients (e.g., soy sauce, noodles, rice, etc.), but not all Asian food sub-categories use soy sauce (like Indian food).

Similarly, not all premium financing methods use the same ingredients either.

Third-Year Financing (3YF) is a very different version of premium financing. One could even argue that for these first two years of the policy, the policy is a *non-financed policy*, only with the *intent* to finance in the third year.

	THIRD-YEAR FINANCING 3YF	FIRST-DOLLAR FINANCING FDF
Peak Collateral:	$187,186	$1,836,774
Annual Premium Borrowed:	$2,025,000 x 8 years	$2,000,000 x 7 Years
Total Premium Borrowed ($):	$16,200,000	$14,000,000
Total Outlay:	**$6,750,000** (partial premium paid)	**$7,661,226** (interest paid)
Initial Face Amount:	$30,500,000	$26,156,622
Low Point Net Death Benefit:	$10,461,437	$10,127,420
Net Death Benefit At Age 89:	$22,562,202	$15,955,144

In summary, compared to the three previous aforementioned premium financing designs, the Third-Year Financing (3YF) platform produces the:

1. Least First-Year Outlay (tied with PEIA)
2. 2nd Least Collateral Required
3. 2nd Least Cumulative Outlay (tied with PEIA)
4. Highest Initial Face Amount
5. Highest Low Point Net Death Benefit
6. 2nd Highest Net Death Benefit At Age 89

FIRST-DOLLAR FINANCING	SECOND-YEAR FINANCING	PARTIAL-EQUITY INTEREST ACCRUAL
FDF	2YF	PEIA
$1,836,774	$0	$286,282
$2,000,000 x 7 Years	$1,500,000 x 6 years	$1,325,000 x 10 years
$14,000,000	$9,000,000	$13,250,000
$7,661,226	**$6,093,293**	**$6,750,000**
(interest paid)	(interest paid)	(partial premium paid)
$26,156,622	$19,616,679	$26,156,622
$10,127,420	$10,108,425	$10,455,260
$15,955,144	$17,177,790	$22,612,063

Chapter 14
Sixth-Year Financing (6YF)

Similar to the spirit of the *Partial-Equity Interest Accrual (PEIA)* model and the *Third-Year Financing (3YF)* model, the *Sixth-Year Financing (6YF)* loan model is intended to give the client a simple experience in that it is designed around a fixed annual contribution in policy years 1-5, then a *similar contribution* in years 6-10, and a loan exit in policy year 11. I say *similar contribution* in years 6-10 for a reason that I shall explain in just a moment.

What inspired me to create this unorthodox loan model was that two carriers that I really like – *Pacific Life* and *Penn Mutual* – abhor any type of interest accrual.

Each carrier has their preferences in terms of how they want to run their premium financing business when it comes to minimum net worth requirements, financial underwriting in general, health underwriting, maximum ages, and an array of other parameters which includes a particular type of loan model.

When it comes to loan models, neither of these carriers like the idea of compound debt accrual, which inspired me to find a solution to accommodate the client's desire to have a *somewhat fixed* annual contribution the way *PEIA* and *3YF* have, but also fit inside of *Pacific Life's* and *Penn Mutual's* design preferences with no interest accrual.

The following two pages will show this *Sixth-Year Financing (6YF)* loan model assuming the client wants to contribute $250,000 per year for a period of 10 years.

This case study assumes a 50-year old male, rated as Preferred Plus, and is built for *accumulation / retirement income*.

SUMMARY OF CARRIER-ILLUSTRATED STATIC RETURNS (DESIGNED
FIRST-DOLLAR FINANCING

Health Rating: **PREFERRED PLUS**   Third Party Loan Payoff Type: **PAR LOAN**

YEAR	AGE	1 TOTAL POLICY PREMIUMS	2 EQUITY PREMIUMS	3 BORROWED PREMIUMS	4 CUMULATIVE PF LOAN BALANCE	5 FINANCING INTEREST RATE	6 INTEREST DUE	7 INTEREST ACCRUED	8 CLIENT CONTRIBUTION
1	50	$250,000	$250,000	$0	$0	0.00%	$0	$0	$250,000
2	51	$250,000	$250,000	$0	$0	0.00%	$0	$0	$250,000
3	52	$250,000	$250,000	$0	$0	0.00%	$0	$0	$250,000
4	53	$250,000	$250,000	$0	$0	0.00%	$0	$0	$250,000
5	54	$250,000	$250,000	$0	$0	0.00%	$0	$0	$250,000
6	55	$680,122	$210,000	$470,122	$470,122	8.20%	$38,550	$0	$248,550
7	56	$680,122	$170,000	$510,122	$980,244	8.20%	$80,380	$0	$250,380
8	57	$680,122	$125,000	$555,122	$1,535,366	8.20%	$125,900	$0	$250,900
9	58	$680,122	$75,000	$605,122	$2,140,488	8.20%	$175,520	$0	$250,520
10	59	$680,122	$20,000	$660,122	$2,800,610	8.20%	$229,650	$0	$249,650
11	60	$0	$0	$0	$0	0.00%	$0	$0	$0
12	61	$0	$0	$0	$0	0.00%	$0	$0	$0
13	62	$0	$0	$0	$0	0.00%	$0	$0	$0
14	63	$0	$0	$0	$0	0.00%	$0	$0	$0
15	64	$0	$0	$0	$0	0.00%	$0	$0	$0
16	65	$0	$0	$0	$0	0.00%	$0	$0	$0
17	66	$0	$0	$0	$0	0.00%	$0	$0	$0
18	67	$0	$0	$0	$0	0.00%	$0	$0	$0
19	68	$0	$0	$0	$0	0.00%	$0	$0	$0
20	69	$0	$0	$0	$0	0.00%	$0	$0	$0
21	70	$0	$0	$0	$0	0.00%	$0	$0	$0
22	71	$0	$0	$0	$0	0.00%	$0	$0	$0
23	72	$0	$0	$0	$0	0.00%	$0	$0	$0
24	73	$0	$0	$0	$0	0.00%	$0	$0	$0
25	74	$0	$0	$0	$0	0.00%	$0	$0	$0
26	75	$0	$0	$0	$0	0.00%	$0	$0	$0
27	76	$0	$0	$0	$0	0.00%	$0	$0	$0
28	77	$0	$0	$0	$0	0.00%	$0	$0	$0
29	78	$0	$0	$0	$0	0.00%	$0	$0	$0
30	79	$0	$0	$0	$0	0.00%	$0	$0	$0
31	80	$0	$0	$0	$0	0.00%	$0	$0	$0
32	81	$0	$0	$0	$0	0.00%	$0	$0	$0
33	82	$0	$0	$0	$0	0.00%	$0	$0	$0
34	83	$0	$0	$0	$0	0.00%	$0	$0	$0
35	84	$0	$0	$0	$0	0.00%	$0	$0	$0
36	85	$0	$0	$0	$0	0.00%	$0	$0	$0
37	86	$0	$0	$0	$0	0.00%	$0	$0	$0
38	87	$0	$0	$0	$0	0.00%	$0	$0	$0
39	88	$0	$0	$0	$0	0.00%	$0	$0	$0
40	89	$0	$0	$0	$0	0.00%	$0	$0	$0
		-$4,650,610	-$1,850,000	-$2,800,610			$650,000	$0	$2,500,000

In column 1, we see the annual policy premium is $250,000 in years 1-5, of which the client pays 100% out-of-pocket, non-financed. We define these payments as *Equity Premiums* (column 2). Then in years 6-10, our algorithm calculates the total policy annual premium, increasing 2.72X to $680,122 (column 1).

Our algorithm then calculates how much of that $680,122 should be paid out-of-pocket by the client (column 2), versus how much should be borrowed from the lender (column 3) in order for the interest due (column 6) plus the partial premium paid by the client (column 2) to equal approximately $250,000 (column 8). At the bottom of column 8, you will see the cumulative client contribution is $2,500,000 (an average annual contribution of

PREMIUM FINANCED LIFE INSURANCE

D TO STAY INFORCE UNTIL AGE 120)   version 236987   Horizon   70.B

At This Index Credit Assumption, Death Benefit Lasts Until Age: **120**   **4 of 9**

PLR: **5.53%**   Initial Gross Policy Face Amount: **$6,020,855**   03/30/23

9 (Cash) GAP COLLATERAL	10 HYPOTHETICAL INDEX CREDIT	11 POLICY DRAWDOWNS	12 GROSS POLICY CSV	13 POLICY CSV NET OF LOANS	14 DEATH BENEFIT NET OF LOANS	15 DEATH BENEFIT +YTY INCOME DRAWDOWN IRR	YEAR	AGE
$0	6.03%	$0	$0	$0	$6,176,199	2370.48%	1	50
$0	6.03%	$0	$124,819	$124,819	$6,339,986	356.06%	2	51
$0	6.03%	$0	$302,406	$302,406	$6,512,725	156.62%	3	52
$0	6.03%	$0	$489,581	$489,581	$6,694,934	93.14%	4	53
$0	6.03%	$0	$686,542	**$686,542**	**$6,886,989**	63.56%	5	54
$0	6.03%	$0	$1,349,109	$878,987	$7,074,469	46.86%	6	55
$0	6.03%	$0	$2,049,973	$1,069,729	$7,260,246	36.29%	7	56
$0	6.03%	$0	$2,791,570	$1,256,204	$7,441,757	29.08%	8	57
$0	6.03%	$0	$3,576,635	$1,436,147	$7,616,735	23.89%	9	58
$0	6.03%	$0	$4,407,823	**$1,607,213**	**$7,782,837**	19.99%	10	59
$0	6.03%	-$2,800,610	$1,718,921	$1,718,921	$7,627,964	16.93%	11	60
$0	6.03%		$1,873,439	$1,873,439	$7,464,525	14.55%	12	61
$0	6.03%	$0	$2,032,128	$2,032,128	$7,292,049	12.65%	13	62
$0	6.03%	$0	$2,195,583	$2,195,583	$7,110,035	11.10%	14	63
$0	6.03%	$0	$2,370,005	**$2,370,005**	**$6,917,955**	9.80%	15	64
$0	6.03%	-$270,068	$2,242,419	$2,242,419	$6,430,250	9.07%	16	65
$0	6.03%	-$270,068	$2,117,898	$2,117,898	$5,915,576	8.43%	17	66
$0	6.03%	-$270,068	$1,997,396	$1,997,396	$5,372,440	7.88%	18	67
$0	6.03%	-$270,068	$1,883,180	$1,883,180	$4,799,268	7.39%	19	68
$0	6.03%	-$270,068	$1,775,099	**$1,775,099**	**$4,194,400**	6.94%	20	69
$0	6.03%	-$270,068	$1,676,399	$1,676,399	$3,556,083	6.52%	21	70
$0	6.03%	-$270,068	$1,589,606	$1,589,606	$2,882,467	6.13%	22	71
$0	6.03%	-$270,068	$1,518,248	$1,518,248	$2,610,558	6.13%	23	72
$0	6.03%	-$270,068	$1,462,160	$1,462,160	$2,418,337	6.18%	24	73
$0	6.03%	-$270,068	$1,421,858	**$1,421,858**	**$2,218,146**	6.22%	25	74
$0	6.03%	-$270,068	$1,388,975	$1,388,975	$1,997,881	6.24%	26	75
$0	6.03%	-$270,068	$1,360,525	$1,360,525	$2,012,090	6.38%	27	76
$0	6.03%	-$270,068	$1,336,447	$1,336,447	$2,033,328	6.50%	28	77
$0	6.03%	-$270,068	$1,316,941	$1,316,941	$2,061,939	6.59%	29	78
$0	6.03%	-$270,068	$1,302,569	**$1,302,569**	**$2,098,656**	6.67%	30	79
$0	6.03%	-$270,068	$1,293,451	$1,293,451	$2,143,754	6.74%	31	80
$0	6.03%	-$270,068	$1,289,207	$1,289,207	$2,196,993	6.80%	32	81
$0	6.03%	-$270,068	$1,291,799	$1,291,799	$2,260,581	6.84%	33	82
$0	6.03%	-$270,068	$1,298,183	$1,298,183	$2,331,206	6.88%	34	83
$0	6.03%	-$270,068	$1,306,088	**$1,306,088**	**$2,406,542**	6.91%	35	84
$0	6.03%	-$270,068	$1,313,268	$1,313,268	$2,484,363	6.93%	36	85
$0	6.03%	-$270,068	$1,317,657	$1,317,657	$2,562,671	6.94%	37	86
$0	6.03%	-$270,068	$1,316,460	$1,316,460	$2,638,707	6.95%	38	87
$0	6.03%	-$270,068	$1,305,821	$1,305,821	$2,708,613	6.95%	39	88
$0	6.03%	-$270,068	$1,281,618	**$1,281,618**	**$2,768,257**	6.95%	40	89

TOTAL INCOME DRAWN: -$6,751,700   (INCOME LASTS UNTIL AGE 89)

$250,000). Obviously the total client outlay is only *approximate* in years 6-10 because it is dictated by the future interest rates in each given year.

The loan is exited in policy year 11 using a participating loan (column 11), and income drawdowns start in policy year 16 at age 65 (also column 11).

This design is the least leveraged of all our premium financing designs, which can be good for a conservative client, but more importantly, it fits within these two carriers' parameters in terms of zero interest accrual.

So despite the reduced leverage, is this design still relevant?

107

Absolutely.

When I designed a non-financed comparison using the same product on the same client, using the exact same client outlay, the *Sixth-Year Financing (6YF)* design generated an annual retirement income drawdown of $270,068 versus the non-financed version only generated an annual income drawdown of $262,623.

	NON-FINANCED	SIXTH-YEAR FINANCING
Annual Cliient Contribution:	$250,000	$250,000
Years Of Contribution:	10	10
Total Outlay:	**$2,500,000**	**$2,500,000**
Annual Income Drawdowns:	$262,623	$270,068
Years Of Drawdowns:	25	25
Cumulative Income Drawn Down:	**$6,565,575**	**$6,751,700**
Year 40 CSV:	$1,080,945	$1,281,618
Total Income + Year 40 CSV:	**$7,646,520**	**$8,033,318**

At first glance, you might say, *"The difference isn't that much to justify the added variables of premium financing."*

When looking at the static returns depicted in a carrier illustration, perhaps that synopsis has merit.

However when evaluating the charges, crediting methodology, and historical volatility of the S&P 500, our proprietary backtesting software analysis tells a very different story.

During the *Best 40-Year Period*, the *Sixth-Year Financing (6YF) Proxy* produces $3,717,286 more income drawn down (60.09% more than the *Non-Financed Proxy*), and after forty years, shows more than double the account value (the *Proxy's* simulated *Cash Value*). Taking into consideration both the income drawn down and the simulated *Cash Value* at the end of year 40, the *Financing (6YF) Proxy* delivers 80.33% more economic value.

BEST 40 YEAR PERIOD ANALYZED	NON-FINANCED	SIXTH-YEAR FINANCING
Cumulative Income Drawn Down:	$6,185,759	$9,903,045
Year 40 CSV:	$4,230,794	$8,881,010
Total Income + Year 40 CSV:	**$10,416,553**	**$18,784,055**
		80.33% MORE

During the *Worst 40-Year Period*, the *Sixth-Year Financing (6YF) Proxy* produces $3,069,040 more income drawn down (63.67% more than the *Non-Financed Proxy*), and after forty years, shows almost double the account value (the *Proxy's* simulated *Cash Value*). Taking into consideration both the income drawn down and the simulated *Cash Value* at the end of year 40, the *Financing (6YF) Proxy* delivers 72.06% more economic value.

WORST 40 YEAR PERIOD ANALYZED	NON-FINANCED	SIXTH-YEAR FINANCING
Cumulative Income Drawn Down:	$4,820,019	$7,889,059
Year 40 CSV:	$1,509,536	$3,001,731
Total Income + Year 40 CSV:	$6,329,555	$10,890,790
		72.06% MORE

One of the main reasons for this disparity – <u>and this is one of the most valuable components of premium financing that I rarely hear people discuss</u> – is that the financed policy's index credit is applied to the *Gross Accumulated Value*, not the *Net Cash Value*, meaning that the *Gross Accumulated Value* is much higher in the financed policy due to the larger premiums that entered the policy. After the third-party loan payoff, the *Gross Accumulated Value* is not affected by the third-party loan payoff. The *Participating Loan* amount stays in the index account, continuing to receive the end-of-year index credit based on the index performance and the floor/cap crediting method.

When the policies – both the *Non-Financed Policy* and the *6YF Policy* – receive the same index credit, the *6YF Policy's* index credit is applied to the larger gross accumulated value. Over time, this larger compounding factor produces more net cash value and higher income drawdowns. As an example, in year 30 during the *Worst 40-Year Period*, the *6YF Proxy's* end of year *Gross Accumulated Value* is $16,015,069 versus only $6,303,114 in the *Non-Financed Proxy*.

When the after-floor/after-cap index credit is applied to a *Gross Accumulated Value* that is almost $10,000,000 greater in the *6YF* model, the *Cash Value* growth far exceeds the *Non-Financed*

Cash Value growth, even with the *Participating Loan* accrued compound debt.

When we explain this mathematical outcome to a client, many clients will ask, *"What if I just invested that $250,000 per year in the market?"*

In my opinion, that is a logical (and intelligent) question to ask. In all of my proposals, I model a backtested analysis that addresses this very question.

I create a hypothetical *Equities & Bonds Account* using the same 121 different 40-Year backtested periods. This *Equities & Bonds Account* is comprised of historical S&P 500 returns for the *Equities* portion of the portfolio, adding an additional 200bps bump to account for approximate S&P 500 dividends (which are not included in the proxy for the life insurance policy).

For the *Bonds* portion of the portfolio, I use historical *10-Year T-Bond* returns.

I also include certain tax assumptions on the portfolio's gains, as well as a reasonable investment fee drag.

In the model below, I assumed 70% of the portfolio has been allocated towards *Equities*, and 30% allocated towards *Bonds*. I assume an *Advisor Fee* of 50bps, a *Fund Manager Fee* of 70bps, and a *Broker Dealer Fee* of 15bps, totaling an all-in investment fee of 1.35%. I also assume the *Equities* gains are taxed at 37.10% and the *Bonds* gains were taxed at only 28.10% (both taxation rates are far below most of our clients' top tier tax bracket).

These are all manual inputs in my software platform, so if an advisor or client wants to see a different fee structure or taxation structure, I can easily accommodate.

During the *Best 40-Year Period*, the *6YF Proxy* generated more than $2,000,000 more retirement income than the *Equities & Bonds Portfolio*. The reason is that when I drew down the same annual income from the *Equities & Bonds Portfolio*, the account was drawn down to $0 by the 38th year. Additionally, the *Sixth-Year Financing (6YF) Proxy* still had an account balance of $8,881,010 by the end of the 40th year, making the total economic benefit 142.53% greater in the *Sixth-Year Financing (6YF) Proxy*.

BEST 40 YEAR PERIOD ANALYZED	EQUITIES & BONDS ACCOUNT	SIXTH-YEAR FINANCING
Cumulative Income Drawn Down:	$7,744,903	$9,903,045
Year 40 CSV:	$0	$8,881,010
Total Income + Year 40 CSV:	$7,744,903	$18,784,055
		142.53%
		MORE

During the *Worst 40-Year Period, Equities & Bonds Portfolio* was also drawn down to $0, this time in the 40th year. The *6YF Proxy* generated 47.85% more economic benefit than the *Equities & Bonds Portfolio*.

WORST 40 YEAR PERIOD ANALYZED	EQUITIES & BONDS ACCOUNT	SIXTH-YEAR FINANCING
Cumulative Income Drawn Down:	$7,366,049	$7,889,059
Year 40 CSV:	$0	$3,001,731
Total Income + Year 40 CSV:	$7,366,049	$10,890,790
		47.85%
		MORE

At the expense of being accused of being too overly detailed, I always want the client (and the advisors I work with) to know that the level of due diligence my process incorporates in every *Premium Financed Life Insurance* case is beyond what any other intermediary of fiduciary will ever do.

Every case I propose is backed up with quantifiable indisputable math. My proposition is void of opinions, pontification, and philosophical wax poetic nonsense.

For the longest time, I took the stance that once a client approaches age 70, premium financing doesn't really provide a substantially greater outcome than a non-financed policy due to policy charges. I would often times say that age 70 is the upper limit of when it makes sense, and the client needs to receive a preferred health rating or better, and even then, it's six-in-one, half-a-dozen in the other.

However I was recently asked to look at a case on a 73-year old male. My initial reaction was, *"He's too old to responsibly premium finance."*

Then I thought to myself, *"I wonder what would happen if I used Sixth-Year Financing (6YF)."*

The *Loan-To-Value (LTV)* would be much healthier due to financing not starting until policy year six. My creative juices started flowing, and I considered that maybe this design could allow a client over the age of 70 being able to still employ some leverage, but do it in a more conservative way, albeit less leveraged.

Sure enough, it worked wonderfully, even in my *backtested/stress-tested* proxy, and created a greater *ROI* for the client than using the same client outlay in a non-financed policy.

This type of creative, outside-the-box thinking, combined with our backtesting software (which I call our *Truth Teller*), produced a great solution where I previously did not think premium financing was a fit.

At the end of the day, there are various degrees of leverage opportunities. Sometimes, the more leverage, the greater potential upside. However sometimes (in the case of *3YF*), using delayed leverage can produce a better outcome.

My goal is to design creative (and often times unorthodox) loan models based on sound mathematical principles, and let the math guide our clients… not emotions, insecurities, greed, stubbornness, or ego.

Chapter 15
The Myth Of Free Life Insurance

I have openly spoken out against over-leveraged, overly-aggressive interest accrual programs in the past, and I continue to do so, simply because:

1. The risk is unnecessary.
2. The risk is unsuitable for most clients.
3. The offer of *free life insurance* is very misleading.

There are very few things in life that are truly free, and life insurance is not one of them. I spoken on several national webinars, as well as spoken at symposiums in front of advisors, CPAs, and attorneys, addressing the irresponsible *free insurance* concept that many premium financing intermediaries have promoted. These models encourage the client to borrow 100% of the premium, accrue 100% of the interest, pay nothing, and simply post collateral.

I liken these offers to the cartoon illustrated below.

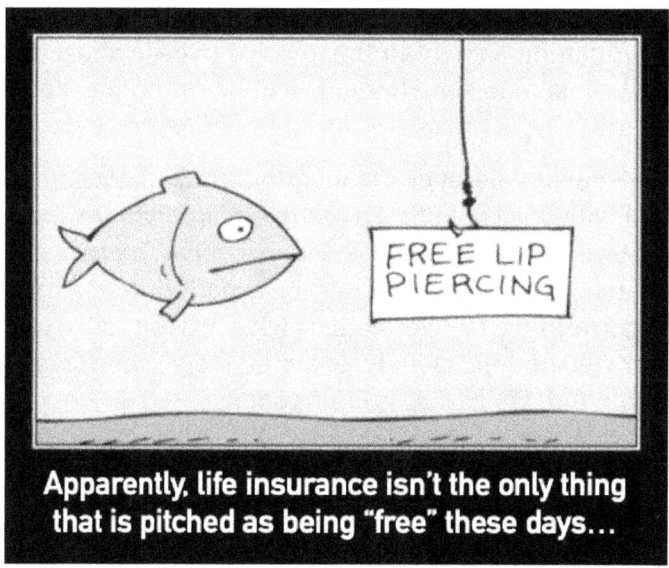

This *free insurance* concept is often times used to attract clients who "don't want to pay" the interest on borrowed premiums in a traditional *First-Dollar Financing (FDF)* arrangement (which usually means they can't really afford the interest due).

I am often asked if there is ever a place for *Premium Financed Life Insurance* programs wherein the client pays *zero out-of-pocket* (or an absurdly small amount of premium and/or interest, then accrues the rest of the interest), knowingly takes on the risk of negative arbitrage potential, and puts a huge amount of collateral at risk.

If the client fully understands the risk – and their liquid net worth could support an upside-down scenario wherein the compounding debt with the third-party lender outpaces the policy value growth – I suppose the client should have the right to do this.

But it reminds me of the mid-2000's where unknowing victims bought homes they couldn't afford under normal circumstances, and recklessly entered negative amortization mortgage loans without truly understanding the risks. Of course we all know what happened in 2008.

I suppose a client that likes higher-risk strategies should be able to make *grown-up* decisions regarding their finances and enter this type of arrangement if they really want to, however for me personally, putting a client in this type of over-leveraged high-risk situation is just not something I feel comfortable doing as an intermediary.

If a client who once claimed that they understood the risks associated with this type of *zero outlay premium financing program* (or an absurdly *low skin-in-the-game premium financing program*) suddenly falls on hard times during a period when the policy's index is performing far worse than what was initially depicted in the carrier illustration, the advisor will likely incur legal liability, especially in today's highly litigious society.

If this type of client decides to litigate and the advisor finds themselves in front of a jury (who are *not* their peers from a financial sophistication standpoint), and they are accused of "tricking" their client into going into massive debt to buy *free insurance* (which turned out to *not* be free after all), and they lost millions of dollars they posted in collateral, the optics are not in favor of the advisor.

Even if the client swears up and down that they can absorb the risk, I still have major concerns about this type of *zero out-of-pocket* premium financing arrangement, largely due to the *optics* – not just the *math*, but the *optics*. Unless you expect the jury to be comprised of mathematicians, insurance actuaries, and sophisticated financial advisors that specialize in cash value life insurance, it is my personal opinion that you should be hesitant to recommend this arrangement to a client.

Perhaps you think I'm being overly conservative in my stance on this issue, and that's okay. We can agree to disagree on the subject of risk, but remember what I alluded to earlier in this book regarding the *Probability Of Risk* versus the *Consequence Of Risk*?

If a person's net worth is below $25,000,000, they likely do not have the liquidity to weather the storm of a *free insurance program gone bad* program, and you – the advisor – will be the first person they blame.

I always say that premium financing is *not* for someone that can't afford the premiums. It is for the type of person that *can* afford the premiums, but believes in the potential benefits of responsible leverage and potential long-term arbitrage between the *Cash Value Growth* and the *Debt Accrual Growth* (both the third-party loan and the Participating Loan.

<u>*Premium Financed Life Insurance* is *re-allocation of assets* strategy for wealthy individuals, not a *get-something-for-nothing* strategy</u>.

On the next two pages, I created a clone of a so-called free insurance program currently being promoted by several of my competitors.

It shows the client putting *zero skin-in-the-game* except for posting outside collateral, with the intention of maintaining a low point net death benefit of $10,000,000 or greater at all times.

YEAR	AGE	1 TOTAL POLICY PREMIUMS	2 EQUITY PREMIUMS	3 BORROWED PREMIUMS	4 CUMULATIVE PF LOAN BALANCE	5 FINANCING INTEREST RATE	6 INTEREST DUE	7 INTEREST ACCRUED	8 CLIENT CONTRIBUTION
1	50	$2,000,000	$0	$2,000,000	$2,000,000	5.70%	$114,000	$114,000	$0
2	51	$2,000,000	$0	$2,000,000	$4,114,000	5.80%	$238,691	$238,691	$0
3	52	$2,000,000	$0	$2,000,000	$6,352,691	5.91%	$375,198	$375,198	$0
4	53	$2,000,000	$0	$2,000,000	$8,727,889	6.01%	$524,778	$524,778	$0
5	54	$2,000,000	$0	$2,000,000	$11,252,667	6.12%	$688,841	$688,841	$0
6	55	$2,000,000	$0	$2,000,000	$13,941,508	6.23%	$868,967	$868,967	$0
7	56	$2,000,000	$0	$2,000,000	$1?,810,475	6.35%	$1,066,928	$1,066,928	$0
8	57	$2,000,000	$0	$2,000,000	$1?,?77,403	6.46%	$1,284,719	$1,284,719	$0
9					?123	6.58%	$1,524,584	$1,524,584	$0
10		**BORROWING RATE DROPS TO**			?	6.70%	$1,789,053	$1,789,053	$0
11						2.50%	$711,894	$711,894	$0
12		**2.50%**				2.50%	$729,691	$729,691	$0
13					?45	2.50%	$747,934	$747,934	$0
14	63	$0	$0	$0	$3?,?5,279	2.50%	$766,632	$766,632	$0
15	64	$0	$0	$0	$3?,431,911	2.50%	$785,798	$785,798	$0
16	65	$0	$0	$0	$32,217,709	2.50%	$805,443	$805,443	$0
17	66	$0	$0	$0	$33,023,151	2.50%	$825,579	$825,579	$0
18	67	$0	$0	$0	$33,848,730	2.50%	$846,218	$846,218	$0
19	68	$0	$0	$0	$34,694,948	2.50%	$867,374	$867,374	$0
20	69	$0	$0	$0	$0	0.00%	$0	$0	$0
21	70	$0	$0	$0	$0	0.00%	$0	$0	$0
22	71	$0	$0	$0	$0	0.00%	$0	$0	$0
23	72	$0	$0	$0	$0	0.00%	$0	$0	$0
24	73	$0	$0	$0	$0	0.00%	$0	$0	$0
25	74	$0	$0	$0	$0	0.00%	$0	$0	$0
26	75	$0	$0	$0	$0	0.00%	$0	$0	$0
27	76	$0	$0	$0	$0	0.00%	$0	$0	$0
28	77	$0	$0	$0	$0	0.00%	$0	$0	$0
29	78	$0	$0	$0	$0	0.00%	$0	$0	$0
30	79	$0	$0	$0	$0	0.00%	$0	$0	$0
31	80	$0	$0	$0	$0	0.00%	$0	$0	$0
32	81	$0	$0	$0	$0	0.00%	$0	$0	$0
33	82	$0	$0	$0	$0	0.00%	$0	$0	$0
34	83	$0	$0	$0	$0	0.00%	$0	$0	$0
35	84	$0	$0	$0	$0	0.00%	$0	$0	$0
36	85	$0	$0	$0	$0	0.00%	$0	$0	$0
37	86	$0	$0	$0	$0	0.00%	$0	$0	$0
38	87	$0	$0	$0	$0	0.00%	$0	$0	$0
39	88	$0	$0	$0	$0	0.00%	$0	$0	$0
40	89	$0	$0	$0	$0	0.00%	$0	$0	$0

This *Over-leveraged Free Insurance Program* uses a $2,000,000 annual premium using a 10-pay design (column 1), borrowing 100% of the premium (column 3), and accruing 100% of the interest (column 7).

If you notice, in order for this magic trick to work, the borrowing interest rate must be dropped to only 2.50% starting in policy years 11-19 in order to payoff the third-party loan in policy year 20 (column 11). The outside peak collateral is $13,598,671 in policy year 11 compared to $1,836,774 in policy year 5 of the *First-Dollar Financing (FDF)* case study I modeled earlier in this book.

For the sake of argument, let's assume the client doesn't mind posting 7.5X more outside collateral. I suppose it is possible that there are clients that have more than enough liquid assets to post as collateral, and they say they don't mind the risk.

PREMIUM FINANCED LIFE INSURANCE

9 (Securities) GAP COLLATERAL	10 HYPOTHETICAL INDEX CREDIT	11 POLICY DRAWDOWNS	12 GROSS POLICY CSV	13 POLICY CSV NET OF LOANS	14 DEATH BENEFIT NET OF LOANS	15 DEATH BENEFIT +YTY INCOME DRAWDOWN IRR	YEAR	AGE
$1,106,716	5.40%	$0	$1,627,596	-$372,404	$26,458,619		1	50
$1,921,250	5.40%	$0	$3,636,433	-$477,567	$26,325,705		2	51
$2,794,129	5.40%	$0	$5,754,385	-$598,306	$26,177,215		3	52
$3,743,654	5.40%	$0	$7,987,865	-$740,024	$26,007,651		4	53
$4,786,109	5.40%	$0	$10,342,739	-$909,928	$25,809,996		5	54
$5,939,966	5.40%	$0	$12,825,212	-$1,116,296	$25,575,877		6	55
$7,224,515	5.40%	$0	$15,442,756	-$1,367,719	$25,296,608		7	56
$8,661,696	5.40%	$0	$18,203,408	-$1,673,995	$24,962,581		8	57
$10,276,368	5		,046,259	$24,562,567			9	58
$12,097,650		**PEAK COLLATERAL**	,497,719	$24,083,356			10	59
$13,598,671			,959,172	$22,294,303			11	60
$12,636,516		**$13,598,671**	,270,074	$21,582,409			12	61
$11,584,230	5.		,521,661	$20,852,718			13	62
$10,431,410	5.40%	$0	$29,954,487	-$710,792	$20,104,784		14	63
$9,171,689	5.40%	$0	$31,598,242	$166,331	$19,338,152		15	64
$7,796,890	5.40%	$0	$33,332,233	$1,114,524	$18,552,354		16	65
$6,297,462	5.40%	$0	$35,162,575	$2,139,424	$17,746,912		17	66
$4,662,560	5.40%	$0	$37,096,178	$3,247,448	$16,921,333		18	67
$2,879,884	5.40%	$0	$39,140,819	$4,445,871	$16,075,115		19	68
$0	5.40%	$35,562,322	$3,986,258	$3,986,258	$13,450,963		20	69
$0	5.40%	$0	$4,437,242	$4,437,242	$11,607,399		21	70
$0	5.40%	$0	$4,938,902	$4,938,902	$10,923,608		22	71
$0	5.40%	$0	$5,497,318	$ 7,318	$10,846,049		23	72
$0				246	$10,727,611		24	73
$0		**LOWPOINT DEATH BENEFIT**			$10,566,090		25	74
$0					$10,359,708		26	75
$0		**$10,359,708**			$11,300,197		27	76
$0				003	$12,305,591		28	77
$0	5.40%	$0	$9,999,305	$ 9,305	$13,379,126		29	78
$0	5.40%	$0	$10,954,269	$10,954,269	$14,524,103		30	79
$0	5.40%	$0	$11,973,830	$11,973,830	$15,743,935		31	80
$0	5.40%	$0	$13,058,816	$13,058,816	$17,039,838		32	81
$0	5.40%	$0	$14,208,822	$14,208,822	$18,411,751		33	82
$0	5.40%	$0	$15,424,758	$15,424,758	$19,861,013		34	83
$0	5.40%	$0	$16,707,159	$16,707,159	$21,388,586		35	84
$0	5.40%	$0	$18,055,838	$18,055,838	$22,994,695		36	85
$0	5.40%	$0	$19,470,427	$19,470,427	$24,679,395		37	86
$0	5.40%	$0	$20,950,688	$20,950,688	$26,442,900		38	87
$0	5.40%	$0	$22,496,965	$22,496,965	$28,286,058		39	88
$0	5.40%	$0	$24,107,013	$24,107,013	$30,207,021		40	89

Under these assumptions, the *Net Death Benefit* does stay above the $10,000,000 low point goal in all years.

However, what happens if the borrowing interest rate does not drop to 2.50%?

Additionally, what happens if the S&P 500 does not produce a positive 5.40% index credit every single year?

What if this client were to have entered this arrangement at the beginning of a recession?

To find answers to these questions, we created a *Proxy* for this design which I will review in the next two pages.

117

# YEAR	AGE	1 TOTAL INDEX CONTRIBUTION	2 CLIENT INDEX CONTRIBUTIONS	3 BORROWED FROM LENDER	4 CUMULATIVE LOAN BALANCE	5 THIRD PARTY LOAN PAYOFF	6 FINANCING INTEREST RATE	7 INTEREST DUE	8 INTEREST ACCRUED
1	50	$2,000,000	$0	$2,000,000	$2,000,000		5.70%	$114,000	$114,000
2	51	$2,000,000	$0	$2,000,000	$4,114,000		5.80%	$238,691	$238,691
3	52	$2,000,000	$0	$2,000,000	$6,352,691		5.91%	$375,198	$375,198
4	53	$2,000,000	$0	$2,000,000	$8,727,889		6.01%	$524,778	$524,778
5	54	$2,000,000	$0	$2,000,000	$11,252,667		6.12%	$688,841	$688,841
6	55	$2,000,000	$0	$2,000,000	$13,941,508		6.23%	$868,967	$868,967
7	56	$2,000,000	$0	$2,000,000	$16,810,475		6.35%	$1,066,928	$1,066,928
8	57	$2,0...					6.46%	$1,284,719	$1,284,719
9	58	$2,0					6.58%	$1,524,584	$1,524,584
10	59	$2,0					6.70%	$1,789,053	$1,789,053
11	60						5.00%	$1,423,788	$1,423,788
12	61						5.00%	$1,494,977	$1,494,977
13	62						5.00%	$1,569,726	$1,569,726
14	63	$0	$0	$0	$32,964,251		5.00%	$1,648,213	$1,648,213
15	64	$0	$0	$0	$34,612,464		5.00%	$1,730,623	$1,730,623
16	65	$0	$0	$0	$36,343,087		5.00%	$1,817,154	$1,817,154
17	66	$0	$0	$0	$38,160,242		5.00%	$1,908,012	$1,908,012
18	67	$0	$0	$0	$40,068,254		5.00%	$2,003,413	$2,003,413
19	68	$0	$0	$0	$42,071,666		5.00%	$2,103,583	$2,103,583
20	69	$0	$0	$0	$0	-$44,175,250	0.00%	$0	$0
21	70	$0	$0	$0	$0		0.00%	$0	$0
22	71	$0	$0	$0	$0		0.00%	$0	$0
23	72	$0	$0	$0	$0		0.00%	$0	$0
24	73	$0	$0	$0	$0		0.00%	$0	$0
25	74	$0	$0	$0	$0		0.00%	$0	$0
26	75	$0	$0	$0	$0		0.00%	$0	$0
27	76	$0	$0	$0	$0		0.00%	$0	$0
28	77	$0	$0	$0	$0		0.00%	$0	$0
29	78	$0	$0	$0	$0		0.00%	$0	$0
30	79	$0	$0	$0	$0		0.00%	$0	$0
31	80	$0	$0	$0	$0		0.00%	$0	$0
32	81	$0	$0	$0	$0		0.00%	$0	$0
33	82	$0	$0	$0	$0		0.00%	$0	$0
34	83	$0	$0	$0	$0		0.00%	$0	$0
35	84	$0	$0	$0	$0		0.00%	$0	$0
36	85	$0	$0	$0	$0		0.00%	$0	$0
37	86	$0	$0	$0	$0		0.00%	$0	$0
38	87	$0	$0	$0	$0		0.00%	$0	$0
39	88	$0	$0	$0	$0		0.00%	$0	$0
40	89	$0	$0	$0	$0		0.00%	$0	$0

BORROWING RATE DROPS TO: 5.00% (vs 2.50%)

This *Proxy* uses an unfavorable historical 40-year period (1971-2010) where in four of the first ten years would have credited a 0.00% index credit (column 14).

This *Proxy* also assumes the borrowing interest rates only drop to 5.00% instead of 2.50% (column 6).

Under these circumstances, column 9 shows an outside peak collateral requirement in year 15 of $19,244,164 (compared to $13,598,671 under the assumption of a static 5.40% index credit and the borrowing rate dropping to 2.50%). Remember, in the *First-Dollar Financing (FDF)* design, the peak collateral was only $1,836,774, and even less in some of my other loan models (which I will discuss later in this book).

But it gets even worse. The so-called *Free Insurance Program* doesn't have the *Net Value* to sustain the charges and *Participating Loan* debt after the third-party lender payoff.

PREMIUM FINANCED LIFE INSURANCE

9 TOTAL CLIENT CONTRIBUTION	10 (Securities) GAP COLLATERAL	11 CALENDAR YEAR	12 INDEX RETURN (GROSS)	13 INDEX RETURN (FLOOR & CAP)	14 INDEX RETURN (EFFECTIVE)	15 ANNUAL INCOME DRAWDOWNS	16 EOY GROSS INDEX ACCUMULATED VALUE	17 EOY INDEX VALUE NET OF INT & EXT LOANS
$0	$1,106,716	1971	12.42%	10.00%	10.00%	$0	$1,950,002	-$299,946
$0	$1,921,250	1972	-1.92%	0.00%	0.00%			17,385
$0	$2,656,459	1973	-41.40%	0.00%	0.00%		FDF: $1,836,774	063,784
$0	$4,009,309	1974	32.00%	10.00%	10.00%			26,431
$0	$5,670,517	1975	25.48%	10.00%	10.00%		PEIA: $286,262	95,503
$0	$6,294,140	1976	-8.28%	0.00%	0.00%			606,577
$0	$6,817,108	1977	6.23%	6.23%	6.23%		2YF: $737,706	819,680
$0	$9,593,229	1978	6.61%	6.61%	6.61%			007,660
$0	$11,135,094	1979	14.76%	10.00%	10.00%		3YF: $187,186	563,790
$0	$12,731,613	1980	-7.40%	0.00%	0.00%			330,278
$0	$12,681,980	1981	3.65%	3.65%	3.65%		$24,150,084	-$4,325,076
$0	$15,642,167	198?					$26,499,897	-$3,399,651
$0	$17,134,948		PEAK COLLATERAL:				$26,442,332	-$4,952,193
$0	$15,822,954						$28,913,686	-$4,050,565
$0	$19,244,164		$19,244,164 (vs $13MM)				$31,727,558	-$2,884,906
$0	$18,025,169						$34,818,601	-$1,524,486
$0	$16,325,943						$34,741,401	-$3,413,840
$0	$14,277,5??	198?	28.41%	10.00%	10.00%		$38,128,894	-$1,939,359
$0	$18,43??						$38,050,359	-$4,021,307
$4,642,83?							$41,771,932	-$4,612,080
$3,971,386			REQUIRES ADDITIONAL:				$44,920,938	-$3,782,275
$5?,854,323			$16,956,582				$49,277,113	-$1,661,260
$4,263,492							$49,634,824	-$4,060,468
$?,924,694							$54,547,014	-$1,833,042
$0	$0	1995		10.00%	10.00%		$59,954,223	$755,164
$0	$0	1996		10.00%	10.00%		$65,909,403	$3,750,391
$0	$0	1997		7.36%	7.36%		$70,714,574	$5,447,611
$0	$0	1998		10.00%	10.00%		$77,729,849	$9,199,538
$0	$0	1999		10.00%	10.00%		$85,436,614	$13,479,787
$0	$0		FDF: $7,661,226	00%			$85,365,799	$9,811,131
$0	$0		PEIA: $6,750,000	00%			$85,282,763	$5,950,361
$0	$0		2YF: $6,750,000	00%			$93,702,006	$10,402,984
$0	$0			00%			$102,939,805	$15,475,832
$0	$0		3YF: $6,093,253	00%			$113,073,708	$21,236,537
$0	$0			1%			$122,733,074	$26,304,044
$0	$0			00%			$134,775,596	$33,525,115
$0	$0			00%			$134,525,648	$28,212,643
$0	$0	2008	-9.37%	0.00%	0.00%		$134,230,226	$22,601,570
$0	$0	2009	7.96%	7.96%	7.96%		$144,538,727	$27,328,638
$0	$0	2010	-0.86%	0.00%	0.00%		$144,135,276	**$21,064,683**

This means the client would have to pay down the *Participating Loan* debt with outside funds (column 9) in the amount of $16,956,582.

The so-called *Free Insurance Program* would *only* cost $16,956,582 in order to net a $10,000,000 low point death benefit.

A similar problem exists if a client only pays interest in the first few years, then accrues 100% of the interest due on the remaining borrowed premiums.

Imagine how your client would feel if this happened to them. Consider how you would feel if you were responsible for endorsing this financial catastrophe.

Imagine buying real estate with a mortgage loan – no money down – and never paying your mortgage payment… and hoping that the real estate appreciates faster than your mortgage debt is compounding when you aren't making any mortgage payments.

Now imagine doing this in 2006, right before the mortgage crisis in 2008. You would never do this, yet THAT is what these *Free Premium Financed Life Insurance* programs are proposing.

The only way to truly know if a *Premium Financed Life Insurance* proposition is properly constructed is to stress-test it using my backtesting software. Otherwise, you have no idea how volatility of interest rates and index credits will affect outcomes.

Chapter 16
The Sin Of Miscalculating Collateral

This is one of the biggest, nastiest, and dirtiest little secrets in the premium financing arena that I haven't heard anyone talk about, which makes it one of the biggest *sins* in this business.

I'm talking about the absurd miscalculation of collateral requirements. I have seen dozens of other premium financing intermediaries' proposals, and it never ceases to amaze me that their calculation of collateral projections is flat out incorrect.

Collateral shortfalls and unexpected collateral calls are perhaps the biggest reasons why *Premium Financed Life Insurance* arrangements fall apart. The client is unpleasantly surprised each year, required to post more outside collateral than anticipated, and the root of the problem starts with working with a premium financing intermediary that doesn't know what they're doing.

As an example, let's say the intermediary is projecting the expected collateral required in policy year six (in their original point-of-sale proposal). They will typically look at the carrier illustration's cash surrender value in policy year six compared to the third-party loan balance in that year. The shortfall between those two numbers is the gap they say needs to be filled with outside collateral.

Here's where the problem starts.

In reality, the lender will calculate their collateral requirement for policy year six during the *middle of the final month* of policy year five. At that point, year five's index credit has not hit yet. It will credit several weeks after the start of policy year six.

But it gets worse.

The *end-of-year* index credit for policy year six won't hit for another thirteen months after that. So if the premium financing intermediary uses the *EOY Cash Surrender Value* in year six to calculate the shortfall in year six, that *Cash Value* amount assumes that policy year five AND policy year six's *end-of-year* index credits have hit, neither of which have.

To properly calculate the collateral requirement in policy year six (in the initial proposal) one must take policy year four's *end-of-year* accumulated value, then add policy year five's premium, then subtract policy year five's charges, then add policy year six's premium, then subtract policy year six's charges, then subtract policy year six's surrender charges. This will give you the actual policy *Cash Surrender Value* at the time the lender will be calculating their collateral requirement.

Most lenders will give this value a 95% advanced rate that the client may apply towards their collateral requirement. This value will then be subtracted from the loan balance projection after the lender funds the sixth-year premium, and that is considered the *gap*.

This *gap* is then filled by some sort of collateral. Most lenders, cash and/or marketable securities are sufficient collateral. If the client uses marketable securities, most lenders will credit an *advanced rate* of 50% to 70%. In other words, if the advanced rate credited is 50%, this means that if the *gap* shortfall is $1,000,000, they will require the client to post $2,000,000 in marketable securities as outside collateral.

Depending on the lender – and depending on the type of securities in the portfolio – the *advanced rate* will vary.

I recently had an advisor send me a proposal they received from one of my *competitors* – another premium financing intermediary. I looked at their collateral projections, and it was appalling how understated they were. To make a very long story short, I rebuilt a clone of their loan model, using their exact policy design and loan assumptions they used. In policy year six, their collateral projection was *$819,407 short*.

Think about this for a moment.

Imagine how would you feel if you were the advisor, and in year six, you had to go to your client and tell them, *"I know you thought you were only going to have post $1.2 million of collateral, but the lender is requiring you to post $2 million... so you need to* *come up with an additional $819,407 more than we thought you'd have to post."*

This is assuming the policy performs as originally illustrated AND it assumes that the interest rates stayed as low as originally illustrated because they were accruing some of the interest due. In their illustration, they started with a borrowing rate of only 3.25%, and though it showed an increasing rate, it tops out at only 4.19%. If the loan rate increases higher than that, the entire proposition turns upside down.

But let's assume everything goes exactly as originally illustrated, and borrowing rates drop back down to 4%. Even under these circumstances, the client will still need to post over *$800,000 more* than they expected to.

This is a disaster waiting to happen, all because the premium financing intermediary didn't properly calculate the collateral need.

It all comes back to managing client expectations.

Under-promise.

Over-deliver.

Ask for the prenup up front, then combine bank accounts once you're married and go all-in with your spouse.

This is the foundation of developing an authentic, trust-and-verified relationship.

Chapter 17
High Interest Rates & Recessions

The *Premium Financed Life Insurance* industry as a whole typically suffers during high interest rate environments because many clients think they should not use leverage during these times. However, this is a very naïve and foolish perspective.

Back in the days of low interest rates, there were plenty of *gun slingers* that were selling the concept of *free insurance*. When interest rates are sub-2%, you can get away with accruing a lot of debt, assuming the policy growth outpaces the 2% in compound interest/debt the client is accruing.

I never played this game.

To me, it was a temporary magic trick that worked under extremely favorable circumstances – low borrowing interest rate assumptions in perpetuity with high index performance in perpetuity – neither of which has never happened historically for any extended period of time.

I have always approached premium financing from an educational standpoint, seeking to help the client understand what the long-term play was.

What I am about to show you is perhaps the key to your success in properly communicating how premium financing actually works to a client.

The entire narrative that I have been clarifying ever since I have been in the premium financing space has been focused on showing a client this historical symbiotic relationship between interest rates and market performance. You can philosophize and pontificate on this subject all day long, however it doesn't truly crystalize in a client's mind until they see indisputable historical data – real numbers – which I can show them.

This is what my entire premium financing proposition focuses on. The biggest concerns that an intelligent client, CPA, or estate planning attorney will have is regarding two things:

1. High Borrowing Interest Rates
2. Poor Policy Performance During A Recession

Let's analyze the worst decade of recession in modern history – the lost decade – the years between 2000-2009. What this upcoming chart shows you is that historically speaking, there has been a two-year lag between a market correction and a significant interest rate adjustment.

We're going to look at historical S&P 500 returns compared to historical borrowing interest rates, assuming the borrowing interest rate is constructed based on historical 1-Year CMT Rates plus a spread of 1.85% (which is what one of our lenders charges).

The year 2000 was the first year of the *Dot Com* bubble bursting wherein the S&P 500 produced a negative 10.14% return. During that year, the borrowing interest rate (based on the loan construction noted above) would have been 7.94%, which is a borrowing rate higher than industry average today in 2024.

However we see that two years later, the borrowing rate decreased from 7.94% in 2000, down to 4.13% in 2002 (a 47.98% decrease). The borrowing interest rate continued to decrease in 2003 down to 3.27%, and again in 2004 down to 3.16%.

YEAR	CALENDAR YEAR	S&P 500 RETURNS (NO DIVIDENDS)		10.00% CAP 0.00% FLOOR		1-YR CMT PLUS 1.85% INTEREST RATE	
1	2000	-10.14%	=	0.00%	vs.	7.94%	
2	2001	-13.04%	=	0.00%	vs.	6.96%	
3	2002	-23.37%	=	0.00%	vs.	4.13%	47.98%
4	2003	26.38%	=	10.00%	vs.	3.27%	
5	2004	8.99%	=	8.99%	vs.	3.16%	
6	2005	3.00%	=	3.00%	vs.	4.64%	46.84%
7	2006	13.60%	=	10.00%	vs.	6.23%	
8	2007	3.52%	=	3.52%	vs.	6.85%	
9	2008	-38.49%	=	0.00%	vs.	5.02%	
10	2009	23.65%	=	10.00%	vs.	2.25%	67.15%

Source: http://www.moneychimp.com/features/market_cagr.htm

2003 was the first positive return year after that three-year negative run, wherein the index produced a positive 26.38% return. Two years later, we see the borrowing rate increased up to 4.64%

in 2005 (a 46.84%increase over 2004). It continued to increase up to a peak of 6.85% in 2007.

However 2007 was the beginning of the mortgage crisis, and as expected, two years later, the interest rate dropped down to only 2.25% (a 67.15% drop from its most recent peak of 6.85% in 2007).

Even more importantly, over time, as you see below using the same starting point of the year 2000 – and an awful sequence of returns – running a 23-year window up until the end of last year (2022) using a 0% floor and a 10% cap, the historical relationship between floor/cap crediting and borrowing interest rates produced a positive arbitrage of 2.23%.

YEAR	CALENDAR YEAR	S&P 500 RETURNS (NO DIVIDENDS)		10.00% CAP 0.00% FLOOR		1-YR CMT PLUS 1.85% INTEREST RATE		POSITIVE OR NEGATIVE ARBITRAGE
1	2000	-10.14%	=	0.00%	vs.	7.94%	=	-7.94%
2	2001	-13.04%	=	0.00%	vs.	6.96%	=	-6.96%
3	2002	-23.37%	=	0.00%	vs.	4.13%	=	-4.13%
4	2003	26.38%	=	10.00%	vs.	3.27%	=	6.73%
5	2004	8.99%	=	8.99%	vs.	3.16%	=	5.83%
6	2005	3.00%	=	3.00%	vs.	4.64%	=	-1.64%
7	2006	13.60%	=	10.00%	vs.	6.23%	=	3.77%
8	2007	3.52%	=	3.52%	vs.	6.85%	=	-3.33%
9	2008	-38.49%	=	0.00%	vs.	5.02%	=	-5.02%
10	2009	23.65%	=	10.00%	vs.	2.25%	=	7.75%
11	2010	12.63%	=	10.00%	vs.	2.30%	=	7.70%
12	2011	0.10%	=	0.10%	vs.	2.14%	=	-2.04%
13	2012	13.29%	=	10.00%	vs.	1.97%	=	8.03%
14	2013	29.43%	=	10.00%	vs.	2.00%	=	8.00%
15	2014	11.54%	=	10.00%	vs.	1.98%	=	8.02%
16	2015	-0.73%	=	0.00%	vs.	2.10%	=	-2.10%
17	2016	9.54%	=	9.54%	vs.	2.46%	=	7.08%
18	2017	19.42%	=	10.00%	vs.	2.66%	=	7.34%
19	2018	-6.24%	=	0.00%	vs.	3.68%	=	-3.68%
20	2019	28.88%	=	10.00%	vs.	4.45%	=	5.55%
21	2020	16.26%	=	10.00%	vs.	3.41%	=	6.59%
22	2021	26.89%	=	10.00%	vs.	1.95%	=	8.05%
23	2022	-19.44%	=	0.00%	vs.	2.25%	=	-2.25%
	Averages:	5.90%		5.88%	vs.	3.64%		**2.23% POSITIVE ARBITRAGE**

Source: http://www.moneychimp.com/features/market_cagr.htm

In 2022, the S&P 500 produced a negative return (-19.44% in this depiction using historical returns sourced from *MoneyChimp.com*). In a premium financed arrangement, there would have been negative arbitrage in that year even with a 0% floor in an IUL.

In today's environment as we start off the year 2024 with borrowing rates the highest they have been in over twenty years, it is possible that we may experience negative arbitrage once again.

But as you see in the two tables on the previous two pages, historically speaking, that type of environment has not lasted for any significant period of time.

Being able to articulate this to a client (and show them indisputable historical numbers) is one of the reasons why my premium financing business has flourished in the midst of a negative arbitrage environment.

This is one of my strongest value propositions, and why financial advisors, CPAs, estate planning attorneys, and family offices have partnered with me as their trusted go-to premium financing intermediary.

Chapter 18
Should PFLI Be Used For Retirement?

One of the most abused areas of *Premium Financed Life Insurance* over the last decade has been using this arrangement to generate a retirement income stream.

The concept is valid, however there are several ways to *cheat the system* and lead a client to believe they can put very little dollars in (sometimes even zero), and magically generate a large income stream that will last them their entire lifetime.

I've seen so many ridiculous *Free Insurance / Free Retirement* programs out there, it boggles my mind that anyone would even fall for this. The biggest problem I have with this concept (and believe me, I have a laundry list of criticisms about this this proposition), is that it attracts the type of client that wants *something for nothing*, and typically the type of people that want *something for nothing* aren't very liquid. They may have high incomes, but without liquidity, if their income dries up in the future due to market conditions, industry changes, or any business cash flow challenges in general, the client won't have the ability to weather the storm, even if it is a short-term storm.

They may be able to make the interest payments today, but they don't have the liquid to make the payments if they lose their income temporarily.

In my younger years – back when I was full of ego – I bought a two-year old *Ferrari 458*. The down payment was $79,000 (which I could afford) and the monthly payments were $3,100 (which I could also afford). My income could easily support the expense, however I wasn't incredibly liquid at that time.

After a year of ownership, the warranty expired, and the dealership offered me an extended warranty. The cost of a one-year extended warranty was $10,000. Ouch. I acquiesced and bought the extended warranty for $10,000 because the *Consequence Of Risk* could have resulted in a five-figure repair expense.

Then a few months later, *Ferrari* announced they were releasing the new *488*, which was going to be *Ferrari's* first twin turbo. I realized my car may greatly appreciate in value because it would be the last naturally aspirated *Ferrari* model, but I also realized that if the new twin turbo version became more desirable, the value of my car might plummet.

If I were truly *wealthy* back then, and I had a fleet of exotic sportscars in my garage that I was collecting (not flipping), if the market value of my car dropped off a cliff temporarily, it wouldn't have been that big a deal. The problem was that I was not wealthy enough (at least not by my standards) to absorb a loss because I was planning on flipping the car within 2-3 years. Long story short, I sold the car after only owning it for only a year and half, and that *pride of ownership* cost me $144,800 to drive my *Ferrari* for only eighteen months ($79,000 down payment + 18 months of $3,100 monthly payments + the $10,000 extended warranty). That doesn't even include the annual service, which I believe was somewhere between $7,000 - $8,000.

In my opinion, I was not a suitable *Ferrari* owner at that time – I was just a braggadocious idiot with a high income. I'd like to think I have matured since then – that I am wiser and less of an egomaniac where I don't feel the need to show off anymore – but I learned a great lesson from that mistake. You see, I could afford the *payments*, but I wasn't liquid enough to afford the *risk*… and *risk mitigation* is what a properly designed premium financing arrangement is all about.

Now, there IS a method of premium financing that CAN be responsibly designed to generate retirement income, and the client doesn't necessarily need to be *wealthy* where their net worth needs to be above $10 million. If their income can support it, and they're in an industry that is semi-recession proof, and they have enough liquid to weather a storm or two… a *Third-Year Financing (3YF)* or even a *Sixth-Year Financing (6YF)* model may be appropriate for them.

As I stated earlier in this book, I own a premium financed policy on my life, and my wife owns a financed policy on her life. I'll explain why we chose to invest in these assets, and perhaps you will glean some perspective on the value of using PFLI in this capacity.

We chose this asset class for several reasons.

I'm not worth $100 million, but I have a relatively high income, and being in the top income tax bracket living in California, I love the idea of parking money in a tax-free asset that accumulates with a stop-loss feature (the 0% floor in my IUL policy).

When I assess whether or not PFLI is suitable for a client in my situation, I break down my adult life into three different stages:

I. My Income-Earning Years.
II. My Retirement Years.
III. My Twilight Years.

During *Stage I* of my adult life – *My Income-Earning Years* – I have a substantial personal overhead with a $2.1 million mortgage on my primary residence, another mortgage on my vacation home in Hawaii, private school tuition for my son, lifestyle expenses, etc. I need to insure the loss of my earned income in the event that I die unexpectedly early. It may sound morbid to think about, but if I fell victim to a fatal car accident, or if I died of cancer, or my life was ended by means of some other common tragedy, my family would not be able to maintain their lifestyle without my income.

The purpose of my policy's death benefit is to provide my family with the liquidity they need to keep our family home and maintain the comfortable lifestyle they enjoy now. I don't *plan* on dying early, but I've never met a cancer victim who *planned* to die early either.

Now, if I am blessed enough to live a nice long healthy life, I will enter *Stage II* of my adult life – *My Retirement Years*. By that time, my mortgage will likely be paid off, my son will be a full-grown independent adult, and my overhead expenses may be lower than they are today. At that point, perhaps I will not need as much death benefit as I need today, so I have the option of drawing down a tax-free retirement income stream from my policy. All the while during *My Income-Earning Years*, the cash value is accumulating tax-free, and is also protected from market crashes due to the 0.00%

floor. These tax advantages and downside protection are extremely appealing to me, and I have found that many clients, CPAs, and estate planning attorneys share a similar perspective on these matters.

I don't know anyone that thinks income tax rates are going to go down. Given this belief, the tax-free growth and tax-free income drawdowns from a *Premium Financed Life Insurance* policy are of tremendous value. From a tax standpoint, it is like a *Roth-For-The-Wealthy*… with a 0.00% floor… with the ability to use leverage in the form of bank capital. That's one heck of a powerful combination. I even own a website – Rothish.com – that explains this concept a series of educational videos. It's not a Roth IRA, but it's taxed like a Roth, so it's kind of *Rothish*.

Then if I'm extremely blessed, I will one day enter *Stage III* of my adult life – *My Twilight Years*. If things go moderately well, even after I take substantial tax-free income drawdowns from my policy, there will still be a death benefit that I will leave behind for my son (and his future grandkids, if I'm so lucky to have them one day).

As I explained earlier in this book, I chose to use our *Second-Year Financing (2YF)* design for my policy and my wife's policy wherein we paid the first year premium out-of-pocket… started financing in policy year two… and we pay the interest due each year. Back then, I had not developed the *Third-Year Financing (3YF)* yet. If I was to start a policy from scratch right now, I would absolutely use the *3YF* design, hands down. For someone in my particular financial situation – mathematically speaking – it is the most efficient loan model.

The chances for outside collateral are perhaps even slimmer than the *Second-Year Financing (2YF)* design that I elected back when I put my policy in force (and my wife's policy). It is built so efficiently, and given where interest rates are today in 2024 – mathematically speaking – it is superior.

I realize that was the second time I used the term *mathematically speaking* within two paragraphs, and that is intentional. At the end of the day, premium financing *should* be a mathematical decision based on indisputable backtesting and stress-testing, comparing every other viable estate planning option, as well as all alternative retirement planning options.

Of course every client is different, so our proprietary backtesting software seeks to uncover the indisputable mathematical truth about what asset construction is the most effective for each specific client.

But like most high-end solutions, it is not just the product chassis or the bank's loan terms wherein the proper due diligence needs to be done. The technician – in this case, the premium financing intermediary – is an integral part of making sure this solution is appropriate and masterfully designed.

There are certainly an abundance of bad actors in this industry, and it is hard for most advisors and consumers to know who they should trust.

Gimmicks and financial magic tricks can mislead clients (and advisors) into believing all that glitters is gold… and sometimes, the sparkle is coming from *fool's gold*.

Chapter 19
Gimmicks To Avoid

When it comes to *Premium Financed Life Insurance,* all that glitters ain't gold. There are several gimmicks that some premium financing designs use to make their value propositions appear greater than what they actually are.

There is no such thing as a free lunch in *Premium Financed Life Insurance.* In addition, there are some gimmicks that I believe lure the wrong type of clients into premium financing, creating an unsuitable arrangement for all parties involved. Not everyone should finance their life insurance premiums, but not because the math doesn't work, and not because the risk is too high.

The reason I say that *Premium Financed Life Insurance* is not a suitable strategy for some people is that it typically requires substantial liquidity – not *stated liquidity* or *future/aspirational liquidity* – but current liquidity.

But if a client's net worth is truly equal to or greater than the carrier's requirements, and their current liquidity is greater than the projected peak collateral in our *Leveraged Hypothetical Synthetic Asset* (the proxy for the premium financed *IUL*) during the 40-year period with the *Worst Compounded Annual Growth Rate...* AND assuming the client doesn't mind posting that amount as collateral (not touching it until the lender's collateral requirement outside the policy value is zero), premium financing is most likely a suitable strategy for them.

However if the client does not have the assets required by the lender to use as collateral, premium financing is just not a viable option for them.

One exception to the rule is that if they can get their own lender to post a *Letter Of Credit* against one of their illiquid assets – like real estate for example – perhaps *Premium Financed Life Insurance* is suitable for them. We do have a few lenders that will accept real estate equity as collateral, however it is still important to make sure the client has the ability to weather short-term financial hardships in the event that their cash flow is negatively affected for whatever reason.

Another exception to the rule is if they use our *Second-Year Financing (2YF)* design or our *Third-Year Financing (3YF)* design I talked about earlier in this book. The chances the client will have to post any sort of significant collateral is slim to none. Keep in mind, they still must have the cashflow to afford the annual contributions, whether they be interest payments or partial premium payments. If their cashflow dries up due to challenges in their business (which certainly happens with all entrepreneurs from time to time), they must have the liquidity to draw from to make their payments/contributions to the plan. If they do not have this liquidity for rainy days, perhaps they should not commit to any sort of premium financing arrangement.

In most cases, when a client says they have the liquidity but just don't want to post it as collateral, it usually means they don't truly have the liquidity they say they do. When this is the case, the first request I most often get from life insurance agents is to use a *High Early Cash Value Rider*. There are several reasons why I am not a fan of using this gimmick.

The first reason is this rider comes at a substantial cost that acts as an eroding factor, making the cash value accumulation suffer over time. As an example, I once reviewed a carrier illustration that assumed a 5.47% index return, $1,000,000 annual premiums, using a *First-Dollar Financing* design. In that design, it showed the policy value paying off the third-party lender in policy year 16 using a *Participating Loan*, plus income drawdowns using the same *Participating Loan* structure.

I built a clone model of this design *not* using the *High Early Cash Value Rider (HECVR)*, and compared it to the version WITH the rider.

This was a *LIRP* design *(Life Insurance Retirement Plan)* built primarily for cash value accumulation and future retirement income drawdowns using participating policy loans.

The policy WITH the *HECVR* produced $414,103 annual drawdowns compared to $453,380 annual drawdowns from the policy WITHOUT the *HECVR*. Over this 40-year period, it was a cumulative difference of $942,648 in total income drawdowns (favoring the design without the *HECVR*).

The reason for this huge disparity in income drawdowns was due to the additional charges the policy incurs with the *HECVR*. In this particular comparison, there were $260,606 in additional charges in the policy due to the *HECVR*.

```
  $3,979,862  Total Policy Charges with HECVR
- $3,719,256  Total Policy Charges without HECVR
    $260,606  Additional Policy Charges with HECVR
```

There is only one reason why someone would ever use a *HECVR* despite the charges creating such a drag on performance: They want to minimize the outside collateral required in the early years.

There is definitely a trade-off that comes with lowering expected collateral requirement amounts in the form of lowering expected income drawdown amounts (and cash value accumulation) when it comes to using a *HECVR* in an *IUL*. In a death benefit-focused design, this rider will also reduce the cash value as well as the death benefit in the later years of the policy.

The decision to give up $942,648 of income (or accept lesser cash value and a lower death benefit) could only be justified if the client had significant illiquid assets that the premium financing lender would not accept as collateral (e,g., real estate farm land, crypto currency, privately held business equity, etc.), and they just didn't have the liquidity.

However for the most part, a client financing a large amount of premium should only be doing so if they have the liquid collateral to do so. In many cases, lenders will allow the client to keep the assets with the current custodian, and if the assets are marketable securities, they can usually keep those assets exactly as they are. So if the client has enough liquid collateral sitting in an investment account that they don't need to touch for 7-10 years anyway, there should not be an client reservation from posting it as collateral on the premium financing loan.

Personally, I think many advisors project their own insecurities about posting collateral onto the client, wherein the client would not have had an issue with posting more collateral if the issue had not been portrayed as a negative element by the advisor. I can't tell you how many times I have seen advisors worry about their client being reticent or upset about an issue, and then I get on a Zoom call with the client, and the client has no problem with the issue.

But perhaps the biggest reason I am not a fan of *HECVRs* has nothing to do with how the drag of the additional charges erode cash value accumulation.

It isn't the chargeback liability for the agent either.

The biggest concern I have regarding *HECVRs* is the message it sends to the client, which is, *"You can exit this arrangement with little or no penalty."*

In theory, this flexibility sounds like a good thing, however using this flexibility as a selling tactic sends the wrong message to the client. Any financial strategy that uses a cash value life insurance policy – financed or not – should be a long-term strategy. If the client enters the arrangement under the wrong premise – focusing on early exit options as an example – a life insurance-based solution is probably not appropriate for this particular type of client.

Though this analogy may be a crass one, if a single person just won the lottery and walked into a bar with a t-shirt that said, *"I'm a $100,000,000 lottery winner, and I'll buy you anything you want,"* I'm not so sure they are going to attract the right person. Now, there is nothing wrong with being a $100,000,000 lottery winner, and there is nothing wrong with buying someone you love anything they want, but if that is the message a person leads with when engaging in a new relationship, it is harder to know what the other person's true intentions are.

Remember, I'm the guy that brought up my requirement of signing a prenuptial agreement on the first date with my wife, only to combine all assets as soon as we got married.

Under-promising then over-delivering, combined with a transparent, full-disclosure approach is what builds long-lasting relationships – authentic relationships.

As a *Premium Financed Life Insurance* intermediary, I believe it is my duty to identify whether or not the client's true intentions are to utilize this strategy for what was designed to do – to provide a long-term wealth building solution, or to be used as an effective estate planning tool. This is not a get-rich-quick scheme, a get-something-for-nothing ploy, or a short-term investment.

I want to know that the client is committed to this as a long-term strategy and that they have the liquidity and emotional fortitude to stay the course and weather any short-term financial storms should they come.

Yes, there is an element of risk in premium financing, but if designed properly, it is no more risky that buying a home with a mortgage loan. In fact, I could make the argument that a well-designed *Premium Financed Life Insurance* arrangement is far less risky because the likelihood of the policy value deteriorating as drastically as the housing market can is infinitesimally smaller.

But as I repeatedly stated over and over in this book, the only way to really understand whether or not a premium financing arrangement is mathematically sound is to create a proxy for the *IUL*, build in pessimistic assumptions, and backtest the design throughout different historical periods of time wherein the index experienced volatility.

I am literally the only premium financing intermediary in the entire life insurance industry that has the ability to do this. In my humble opinion, this is the only true test of whether or not a *Premium Financed Life Insurance* arrangement is a prudent financial strategy.

Chapter 20
The History Of The Author

So why should you listen to me?

A wise man once said, *"If you don't know the history of the author, then you don't know what you're reading."*

That being said, I will share with you my background, how I got into this highly specialized line of work, as well as the current scope of my business.

When most people hear that I finance $50 million to $100 million life insurance policies for uber-wealthy clients, they often think I grew up around extremely wealthy people. Perhaps they think I spend my time at private country clubs sipping on overpriced cocktails holding my martini glass with my little pinky finger up in the air, hobnobbing with the likes of *Thurston Howell, III*.

Nothing could be further from the truth. I started my career in the insurance industry in 2003 after I decided to end my career as high school teacher in Hawaii. I moved back to Long Beach, California where I was born and raised and entered the insurance industry at age thirty-one. I got my start in the employee benefits arena, selling health insurance programs to small companies, and let me tell you, it was not as easy as I thought it was going to be.

The *California State Department of Insurance* issued my insurance license on January 3, 2003, and to say that 2003 was a *rough year* would be the understatement of a lifetime. I first solicited people I knew – my friends and family – and tried to get them to buy insurance from me. To my chagrin, most of them declined my offers. So I started cold calling businesses, and as you can probably imagine, my results were even more dismal. Nobody wanted to talk to me, and perhaps I couldn't blame them, for I was a brand new insurance agent with no experience.

My 2003 personal tax return showed a total income of $277 for the entire year. I actually have a copy of it framed on the wall of my office.

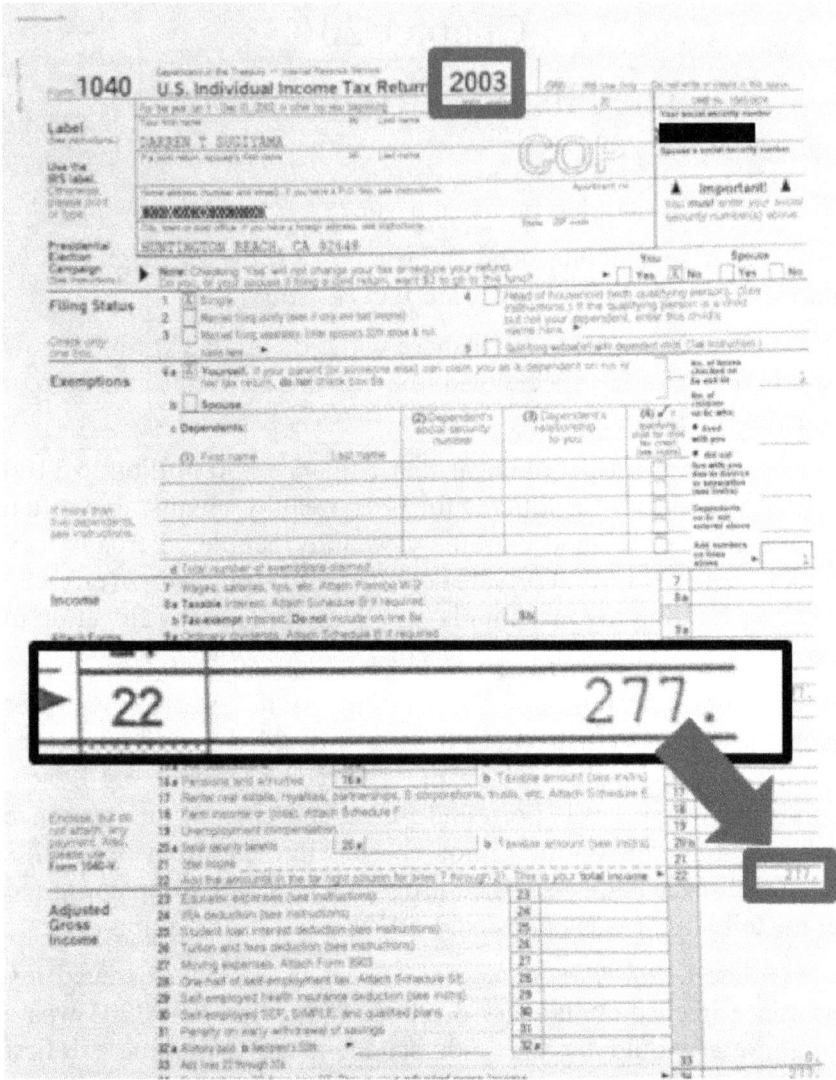

Darren Sugiyama's 2003 Personal Tax Return showing an income of $277 for the year.

I think it's important for all of us to remember where we came from. It keeps us humble and grounded, regardless of how much success we may have achieved in our lives. Looking at my 2003 tax return on my wall every day is a great reminder that I didn't always have the caliber of clientele I have today.

After spending my first year in the insurance industry trying to emulate what other successful insurance agents have done (and failing miserably at it), I decided to do something extremely unconventional.

I took a step back – taking an outsider's view of the industry – and started designing an entirely different client proposition. I took a strategy that large corporations were using in their employee benefit packages, scaled it down, and re-engineered it into a new platform for small businesses that didn't have access to big company benefits.

Everyone in the insurance industry told me that my vision of reinventing the wheel was a bad idea, but after two years of recalibrating my platform based on what I *thought* small company employee benefits *could* be, my unconventional methodology began to get traction. I took my idea to two different *TPAs (Third-Party Administrators)* and built a white-labeled semi-self-funded strategy using supplemental insurance products from specialty carriers in conjunction with the major medical carriers.

Five years into my insurance career, I had built one of the fastest growing employee benefits firms in the industry. My firm, *Apex Outsourcing* was the #1 producing firm in the country for *Kaiser Permanente, HealthNet,* and *Colonial Life* concurrently; the #2 firm in the State of California for *Aetna*; top 30 in California for *Blue Cross*; and by my seventh year in the business, my firm had topped over $37 million in annual recurring premium.

I actually wrote a book about it called **How I Built A $37 Million Insurance Agency In Less Than 7 Years**, and it has become one of the insurance industry's most notorious books ever published. In fact, if you search the term *Insurance Agency* on *Amazon*, the first edition of my book pops up on the first page and has more reviews than any other book in its category. I have since written a *Second Edition* version of this book as well.

When I originally wrote that book, I was in my mid 30's and I met a so-called financial advisor that implemented a very elaborate life insurance-based financial strategy within my company. To make a very long story short, his recommendations ended up losing me $930,000 within a three-year period of time.

This experience absolutely enraged me, but as angry as I was, I was far more embarrassed. I thought I was a reasonably smart person, but taking that kind of financial loss made me feel naïve. It made me feel violated. It made me feel stupid.

I spent the next year obsessively studying every life insurance product in the market, learning about how each product chassis was built, how the crediting methods work, how the underlying investments work, and how the policy charges work. I took those lemons I was dealt and decided to make a lemonade factory.

I ended up writing another book called ***Ouch: How My Financial Advisor Lost Me $930,000 In Three Years***. The concepts I wrote about in that book served as the foundation of building my second insurance agency – *DaVinci Financial* – this time specializing in life insurance for business owners. We used that book to teach our clients how to avoid what happened to me.

I built *DaVinci* into a sizable firm in Orange County, California that at one point housed over forty life insurance agents and financial advisors, plus I also built additional satellite offices in Las Vegas, Nevada; Hartford, Connecticut; Seattle, Washington; Dallas, Texas; and Manhattan, New York. Eventually, we became responsible for over 24% of all the life insurance policies sold in Orange County, California for *Pacific Life* in 2017, over 29% for *Penn Mutual* in 2018, and over 38% for *Penn Mutual* in 2019.

I was running both *Apex* and *DaVinci* concurrently, and in 2016, I started building *Lionsmark Capital*, my premium financing intermediary firm. *Lionsmark* quickly became known as the most mathematically-sound premium financing intermediary in the insurance industry. At that time, I had a business partner, but one thing I have learned over time is that sometimes the people that start out with you don't finish with you. As the great samurai warrior – Miyamoto Mushashi – once said, *"Never be saddened by a separation."* In retrospect, the dissolution of that partnership was the best thing that could have happened to me. It forced me to innovate on my own, and as fate would have it, I ended up taking *Lionsmark Capital* to places it would have never gone had I not been the sole *admiral* guiding my ship.

Entering the niche space of premium financing back in 2016 – especially as an intermediary – was a counter-intuitive thing for me to do by most people's standards. I already had two successful multi-agent insurance agencies – one employee benefits firm and one life insurance firm – and so doubling down on building a premium financing intermediary firm was a big decision for me. But I identified two glaring deficiencies in the premium financing industry – two vitally important things that every client and advisor was silently begging for: *Transparency* and *Client Education.*

I felt it was time for me to innovate again – to reinvent another *new wheel.* Most people thought I was crazy for making this shift, but similar to my two previous insurance ventures, I was confident that my unorthodox approach and fresh perspective could disrupt the entire industry. I didn't want to merely build a *better* version of a premium financing intermediary firm. I wanted to create an entirely different client experience, as well as give advisors a completely new intermediary experience. As I said, I wanted to reinvent a *new wheel.*

Back in 2013, I started building an algorithmically-based software solution that could backtest and stress-test *Indexed Universal Life (IUL)* insurance policies' crediting methods. I started out by using these backtesting models in *DaVinci*, but I wanted to be able to expand my software solution into modeling premium financing arrangements, especially during times of volatility. No one in the life insurance industry was doing anything like this, and even to this day, no one has been able to replicate it.

I went to all the *advanced markets* attorneys at the major insurance carriers and explained what I was doing because I wanted to make sure I wasn't violating any compliance regulations. I emphatically clarified that my models were not recreations of *insurance policy illustrations*, rather they were hypothetical synthetic models that would help educate clients on how different elements of these products actually work; things like floors, caps, charges, and multiplier bonuses.

The spirit of my work has always been rooted in *client education* – probably a subconscious effort to continue my teaching career in a reimagined way.

When I first started implementing these mathematically-based models in premium financing back in 2017, *Lionsmark* primarily used a direct-to-consumer business model whose clientele was mostly small business owners. I felt that this was a great way for me to launch *Lionsmark* because I could control 100% of the point-of-sale process, refining our reimagined way of positioning premium financing. I had two in-house marketing agents that cold called business owners in thirty different states.

We used a virtual point-of-sale business model, selling over the phone, long before *COVID-19* and *Zoom*, back when people told me that *no one* would buy *Premium Financed Life Insurance* over the phone, never having met us. The reality is, people told me the same thing about employee benefits, yet *Apex* sold group health insurance over the phone and email, and *DaVinci* sold life insurance using a virtual model as well. With *Lionsmark*, we used the same business model of *virtual selling* I perfected back in 2009 using an auto-dialer I custom built in-house. My system dialed 400 dials per day per agent.

I still remember the first premium financing case we wrote. A client in Nebraska opted for our platform we used to call *Leveraged Index Arbitrage*, wherein the client paid the first year premium out-of-pocket, and financing started in either year two or year three. This client sent us a first-year premium check for $400,000 – to a firm he's never heard of – to an agent he's never met that cold called him out of the blue. At that point, I realized my unconventional model of doing business *virtually* in an industry that was used to doing things face-to-face would work once again, even with the high net worth market. Of course we all do *Zoom* meetings now, but back in 2017, this was unheard of.

Once word started getting out that we had a superior technology-based backtesting and stress-testing method – as well as a proprietary way to mitigate client risk – other advisors began to inquire. My *ex-competitors* became my *referral sources,* and I am now one of their most trusted resources when it comes to interfacing with their most valuable clients.

By 2018, my reputation in the industry began to evolve from being *a guy that builds large insurance agencies*, to *THE guy that does premium financing the RIGHT way*.

I started receiving requests to speak at industry events as a premium financing expert. The first major speaking engagement happened on November 7, 2018 where I was asked to speak at *Simplicity Life's Premium Financing Symposium* in Houston, Texas.

I still remember hearing the *Senior Vice-President of Premium Financing* from a large bank explain that they only lend annual premiums of $1,000,000 or greater, which resulted in a total loan facility of $7,000,000 to $10,000,000.

I remember thinking to myself, *"Whoa, those are some big policies."* Back then, our average-sized policies were about a third of that. Fast forward to my current client demographic, a $1,000,000 annual premium with a $10,000,000 loan facility has become my *new normal*.

On March 19, 2019, I spoke from stage at *FFR's Spring Symposium* at *The Montage Resort* in Laguna Beach, California on how I approach premium financing in a completely different and reimagined way.

Darren Sugiyama speaking at FFR's 2019 Spring Symposium.

That *FFR* speaking engagement was a major pivotal moment for me because of the exposure it gave me to a larger audience: Advisors, Carrier Executives, Wholesalers, and Distribution Partners. It really cemented my reputation as being an expert in the premium financing arena, sending a message to the entire industry that I was now a force to be reckoned with.

Later that month, I was invited to speak at *Penn Mutual's Advance Planning Council* in Irvine, California as the subject expert on premium financing, and the very next month in April, I spoke at another event at their regional office in Chicago, Illinois.

Later that year in August 2019, *Nationwide* hosted a premium financing symposium at their corporate office in Columbus, Ohio, and *Lionsmark Capital* was the only *non-Nationwide* presenter at their entire symposium.

Later that year, I wrote a book called *The Definitive Book On Premium Financing* that quickly became, well, the definitive book on premium financing.

In the midst of the 2020 pandemic, *Pacific Life* held their *National Symposium* virtually, and I was a featured speaker as the subject expert on *IUL* multipliers.

I was chosen to speak about the charges and crediting methodologies used in their *PDX2* and *PIA6 IULs* alongside Stephan Mitchell – the *Assistant Vice President of Product Marketing at Pacific Life* at that time – who is someone that I have always had an immense amount of respect for as an *IUL* expert and product technician.

I believe *Pacific Life's* decision to select me as a speaker for this nationally broadcasted event was largely due to the sophistication of my backtesting modeling capabilities.

I have been the featured speaker on premium financing at seminar and webinar events sponsored by other carriers including *John Hancock* and *Ohio National*, as well as other BGAs and producer groups like *AEG, Alpine Brokerage, BGA Insurance, Center for Tax Strategies & Resources, CPS, Elite Resource Team, The Producers Group, Redwood Tax Specialists,* and *Peloton* (an *IMO* that supports over 20 different *BGAs*).

Now, I know the previous few pages of this book probably sounded like shameless self-promotion and braggadocio (and perhaps it was), however I felt it was important to establish my background and credibility on this topic. As I said at the beginning of this book, a wise man once said, *"If you don't know the history of the author, then you don't know what you're reading."*

As my reputation in the life insurance industry grew, I began receiving strong endorsements from insurance carriers, investment broker-dealers, *IMOs*, and *BGAs*, publicly saying that *Lionsmark Capital* should be a financial advisor's *Hired Gun Of Choice* when it came to premium financing. This level of endorsement gave me the credibility I needed to grow my firm exponentially.

The financial professionals that I do business with today come from a variety of different disciplines, including financial advisors, CPAs, estate planning attorneys, family offices, and of course, life insurance agents. These professionals rely on my firm to not only secure the lender capital for their high-end clients, but also to articulate how our algorithmically-designed platforms mitigate risk in a way that no other premium financing intermediary can.

If you go to my website – *LionsmarkCapital.com* – and click on *About Us*, you can watch interview videos of some of the top financial advisors, CPAs, attorneys, and carriers talking about their experiences doing business with me.

In closing, I will reiterate the importance of not only understanding *The Probability Of Risk*, but more importantly, *The Consequence Of Risk*. If you are a client that is considering *Premium Financed Life Insurance* as a wealth building or generational wealth preservation strategy, you owe it to your family to insist that the premium financing intermediary you decide to work with is able to do the due diligence I have described in this book and model a range of scenarios with volatility and pessimistic assumptions.

And if you are a life insurance agent or financial advisor that is considering recommending *Premium Financed Life Insurance* to your clients, I cannot emphasize enough the importance of working with an intermediary that truly understands these concepts and can articulately communicate these variables to your clients.

    Making a big life insurance sale is great, but it is far more important to make sure you are doing the right thing for the client, and if you can mathematically prove that your recommendation is not only appropriate, but superior to all other available alternative options, you are providing an invaluable service to your clients.

For more information about Darren Sugiyama, visit:
www.DarrenSugiyama.com

For more information about Lionsmark Capital, visit:
www.LionsmarkCapital.com

This is the 11th book Darren Sugiyama has authored, with many of his published works being distributed in Australia, Brasil, Canada, Croatia, Czechoslovakia, Denmark, India, Italy, Japan, New Zealand, Norway, Singapore, Sweden, the United Kingdom, and the United States of America. Darren lives with his wife Emilia and his son Estevan in Orange County, California

www.ingramcontent.com/pod-product-compliance
Lightning Source LLC
Chambersburg PA
CBHW070436180526
45158CB00019B/1460